SKILLS DEVELOPMENT

READING	LISTENING	SPEAKING	WRITING
Blind date *Looking for love* A newspaper organizes a date between two of its readers. How will they get on? (jigsaw) p10	**My oldest friend** Three people talk about their oldest friend p9 **Blind date** Sally and Dominic talk about their date p10	**Discussion** Talking about your friends p9 **Exchanging information** Talking about the couple on a blind date p10 **Social expressions** Acting out conversations p13	**Describing friends** Symbols for correcting mistakes ~~enjoing~~ Sp Writing about your best friend p56
The happiness quiz *How happy are you?* Find out how happy you are, and what you can do to make yourself happier p18	**Song** *Money* – the best things in life are free p18 **Getting on with your neighbours** Two neighbours gossip about each other. Do they see things in the same way? p20	**Discussion** What's most important to you – money, job, health …? p14 **Exchanging information** Ask and answer questions about three people p16 **Describing** My perfect day p17	**Writing a postcard** Adjectives *great, wonderful, amazing …* Writing a postcard about a holiday p57
The flight attendant who lost his cool *Stephen Slater* Day-by-day newspaper articles as a story breaks, goes global, then dies p26	**The news** Radio news items p25 **Dictation** Transcribing a news story p25	**Narrating** Retelling a news story p24 **Project** Research a news story that interests you – tell the class p25 **Discussion** Famous for fifteen minutes p26	**Narrative writing** Expanding sentences in a story *… a burglar broke into a large, expensive house….* Picture story *A fishy tale* Comparing stories p58
Unusual places to eat *No ordinary place to eat!* Three extraordinary restaurants (jigsaw) p34	**Our diet** A couple talk about their diet p31 **Unusual places to eat** People talk about their experiences of eating in extraordinary restaurants p34	**Discussion** A good diet p31 **Exchanging information** Talking about a restaurant p34 **Roleplay** Acting out a conversation p36	**Writing an email** Linking words *but, although, however so, because* Writing an email to a friend p60
Hope for the future *The girl with two families* A girl from Belarus whose life changed when she visited Ireland p42	**How does it feel to be 20-something?** Three people talk about what it's like to be in their twenties p41	**Describing** Talking about someone in their twenties p41 **Discussion** Living at home/leaving home p41 **Roleplay** An interview with Palina p42	**Writing for talking** My dreams for the future *In five years' time I would like to …* *One day I hope to …* Writing about future plans – tell the class p61
Multicultural London *The world in one street* Four people from different cultures talk about living in the most cosmopolitan city in the world (jigsaw) p50	**My family** People talk about who they are like in their family p49 **What's on?** Deciding what to do in London p53	**Talking about you** Who are you like in your family? p49 **Exchanging information** Talking about an immigrant p50 **Project** Research the life of someone from a different country – tell the class p50	**Describing my hometown** Relative pronouns *who/that/which/where* Pittsburgh – the town where I was born Writing a description of your hometown p62

1 Getting to know you

Questions • Tense revision • Right word, wrong word • Social expressions

STARTER

1 Match the questions and answers.

Where were you born?	Two years ago.
What do you do?	Twice a week.
Are you married?	In Scotland.
Why are you learning English?	I'm a teacher.
When did you start learning English?	No, I'm not.
How often do you have English classes?	Because I need it for my job.

2 **T 1.1** Listen and check. Ask and answer them with a partner.

WHERE DO YOU COME FROM?
Tenses and questions

1 **T 1.2** Listen to **Anton Kristoff**. Where does he come from? Say one thing you can remember about his present, past, and future.

2 Complete the text about Anton with verbs from the boxes.

present	past	future
~~come~~	was born	'm going back
earn	arrived	'm going to study
have	had	
like	moved	
'm living	didn't speak	
'm working		
'm saving		

T 1.2 Listen again and check.

3 Work with a partner. Make sentences about him. Begin like this:

Anton comes from Canada, but now he's working in ...

4 Write one sentence each about your present, past, and future. Read them aloud to the class.

Anton Kristoff
from Toronto, Canada

present 'Hi! I'm Anton. I ¹___come___ from Canada, but at the moment I ²_____ here in New York. I ³_____ as a bike messenger. I really ⁴_____ New York, it's the center of the universe and it's very cosmopolitan. I ⁵_____ friends from all over the world. I ⁶_____ about $100 a day in this job. That's good money. I ⁷_____ money for my education.

H ay

Pre-I

Part A

dition

Liz Soars

OXFORD

UNIVERSITY PRESS

CONTENTS   LANGUAGE INPUT

5 Look at the photo of **Rowenna Lee**. Where does she come from? What do you think her job is?

6 [T 1.3] Listen to Rowenna. What can you remember about her present, past, and future?

present	past	future

7 Complete the questions about Rowenna. Ask and answer them with a partner.

1 Where _does she_ live? Who with?
2 What _____ do?
3 What _____ doing at the moment?
4 When and why _____ to England?
5 How long _____ study law?
6 How much money _____ borrow from the bank?
7 How many children _____ have?
8 Why _____ excited?

[T 1.4] Listen and check. Practise again.

past 'I ⁸_____ in Toronto, but my parents are from Bulgaria. They ⁹_____ to Canada thirty years ago. When they first ¹⁰_____, they ¹¹_____ any English. They worry about me. Last month, I ¹²_____ a bad accident on my bike, but I'm fine now.

future 'Next September, I ¹³_____ home to Toronto and I ¹⁴_____ for a Master's degree, and then I hope to get a good job.'

Rowenna Lee
from Melbourne, Australia

GRAMMAR SPOT

1 Find examples of present, past, and future tenses in [T 1.3] on p63.

2 Name the two tenses in these sentences. What is the difference between them?

He **lives** in Toronto.
He**'s living** in New York at the moment.

3 Match the question words and answers.

What ...?	Because I wanted to.
Who ...?	Last night.
Where ...?	$10.
When ...?	A sandwich.
Why ...?	For two weeks.
How many ...?	In a small village.
How much ...?	My brother.
How long ...?	The blue one.
Whose ...?	It's mine.
Which ...?	Four.

▶▶ Grammar Reference 1.1 – 1.3 p73

PRACTICE

Asking questions

1 Read the interview with Serkan, a Turkish student in England. Complete the questions with question words from the box.

what	where	who	why	which
how often	how much	how many		

I Hi, Serkan. Nice to meet you. Can I ask you one or two questions?

S Yes, of course.

I First of all, ¹_____ do you come from?

S I'm from Istanbul in Turkey.

I And ²_____ are you here in England?

S Well, I'm here mainly because I want to improve my English.

I ³_____ English did you know before you came?

S Not a lot. I studied English at school, but I didn't learn much. Now I'm studying in a language school here.

I ⁴_____ school?

S The Shakespeare School of English.

I A good name! Your English is very good now. ⁵_____'s your teacher?

S Thank you very much. My teacher's called David. He's great.

I ⁶_____ did you do back in Turkey?

S Well, actually, I was a teacher, a history teacher. I taught children from 14 to 18.

I ⁷_____ children were in your classes?

S Sometimes as many as 40.

I Goodness! That's a lot. ⁸_____ do you go back home?

S Usually I go every two months, but this month my brother is coming here. I'm very excited. I'm going to show him round.

I Well, I hope your brother has a great visit.

2 **T1.5** Listen and check. Find examples of present, past, and future tenses in the interview. Roleplay the interview with a partner.

Who's or Whose?

3 *Whose* and *Who's* sound the same.
T1.6 Listen and repeat.

> *Whose* … asks about possession.
> *Who's* = who is
> **1** 'Whose phone is ringing?'
> 'It's mine.'
> **2** 'Who's calling?' 'It's my brother.'

4 Work with a partner. Choose the correct word.

1 'Who's / Whose brother is coming to stay?'
'Serkan's brother.'

2 'Who's / Whose talking to Serkan?'
'I think it's a reporter.'

3 'Who's / Whose dictionary is this?'
'It's Serkan's.'

4 'Who's / Whose going to Ben's party?'
'I'm not.'

5 'Who's / Whose is that expensive car?'
'It's my neighbour's.'

6 'Do you know who's / whose bag this is?'
'It's mine.'

5 **T1.7** Listen to the sentences.

> If the word is *Whose?* shout **1**!

> If the word is *Who's?* shout **2**!

Questions about you

6 Each of these questions has one word missing. Write it in.

1 What *do* you like doing in your free time?

2 Do you like listening music?

3 What kind music do you like?

4 What did you last weekend?

5 What you doing tonight?

6 What are you going do after this lesson?

7 How many languages your teacher speak?

8 What your teacher wearing today?

T1.8 Listen, check, and repeat.

7 Ask and answer the questions with a partner.

T1.9 Listen and compare.

LISTENING AND SPEAKING
My oldest friend

1 Write down the names of some of your friends.

- Why do you like them?
- When did you first meet them?
- Who is your oldest friend?

Discuss your list with a partner.

2 Three people are talking about their oldest friend. Look at the pictures. Who are they talking to? Who are they talking about?

3 **T 1.10** Listen to their conversations. When and where did they meet their oldest friend? What did they like about them? Make notes after each conversation.

Pete

Judy and Kenny

Damian and Toby

Kenny _____
_____
_____ .

Damian _____
_____
_____ .

Katie _____
_____
_____ .

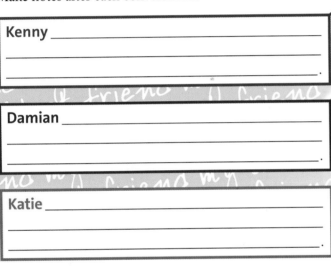

Zac

4 **T 1.10** Listen again. Answer the questions about the people.

1 Who has a lot of friends on Facebook? How many?
2 Whose mums met before they were born?
3 Who's going to travel the world with a friend?
4 Whose oldest friend lives in Canada?
5 Who's talking to their oldest friend?
6 Who doesn't have many friends?
7 Which friends don't see each other very often?
8 Who named his son after the friend?
9 Whose friend is like a sister?
10 Whose brother is boring?

Check your answers with a partner.

Katie and Beth

Katie and Beth

5 Put the words in the right order to make sentences about the people.

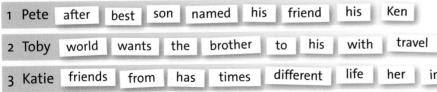

1 Pete | after | best | son | named | his | friend | his | Ken

2 Toby | world | wants | the | brother | to | his | with | travel

3 Katie | friends | from | has | times | different | life | her | in

▶▶ **WRITING** Describing friends *p56*

READING AND SPEAKING
A blind date

1 In a survey, 10,000 couples were asked how and where they first met. How do you think most couples meet? Look at the chart and match a line with a percentage.

How did they meet?	%	
at school or university	12%	
at work	15%	20%
at a bar or club		5%
online	8%	
through friends		13%
through family	4%	
a blind date		1%
while shopping	22%	
none of these		

T 1.11 Listen to the survey results. Did anything surprise you? Talk about couples you know. How did they meet?

2 Each week the *Guardian* newspaper organizes a blind date between two of its readers. Look at the pictures and read the introduction.

- Who are the people? How old are they?
- What are their jobs?
- Where did they meet?

3 Work in two groups.

Group A Read what **Sally** says about **Dominic**.
Group B Read what **Dominic** says about **Sally**.

Answer the questions in your group.

1 Were they both nervous when they met?
2 How does he/she describe her/him?
3 What did they talk about?
4 Why was she/he embarrassed?
5 What did they use to eat their food?
6 What were the best things about him/her?
7 What didn't he/she talk about?
8 How did the evening end?
9 How did she/he travel home?

4 Compare answers with someone from the other group. What do Sally and Dominic have in common? What don't they have in common?

What happened next?

5 Do you think Sally and Dominic will meet again? Take a class vote.

6 **T 1.12** Listen to Dominic and Sally. What did they do? What are they doing now? What are they going to do?

Blind date

This week

Sally Fox, 25, tennis coach meets Dominic Evo, 29, actor.

They met in a Chinese restaurant called *Ping Pong*. Will they ever meet again?

Sally
talking about Dominic

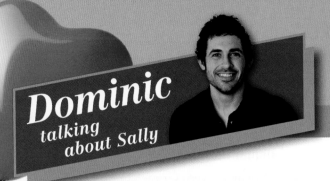

Dominic
talking about Sally

First impressions? He was friendly, tall, and attractive. We laughed together from the start, I think because we were both a bit nervous.

What did you talk about? So many things – places we want to travel to, such as South America. Sport, of course. Unfortunately Dom doesn't play much sport, but he's going to run the marathon this year. His acting – I don't often go to the theatre so I didn't have a lot to say.

Any difficult moments? I couldn't decide how to greet him when we first met. I shook his hand and he tried to kiss my cheek. That was a bit embarrassing, but we laughed about it.

Good table manners? Yes, very. He couldn't use chopsticks, but he tried.

Best thing about him? He was chatty and funny. He didn't just talk about himself, he asked me questions. It was nice to meet a guy who wasn't crazy about football.

Did you go on somewhere? Just to the square next to the restaurant. There was a piano with a notice 'Please play me' – so Dom did. He can play the piano very well. It was a great way to end the evening. He lives out of town, so he went to get his train.

Marks out of 10? I liked him more and more as the evening progressed. 8.

Would you like to meet again? Maybe. We swapped numbers, so we'll see.

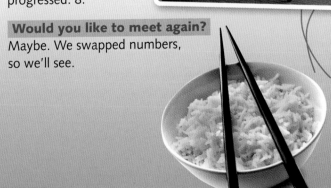

First impressions? She smiled a lot. She has a lovely smile and amazing green eyes. I think she was a bit nervous. I loved her red dress – it was very red indeed.

What did you talk about? Everything – travel, we both want to visit Chile; cooking, I love it, Sally hates it; sport, I hate it, Sally loves it, but I am training to run the marathon for charity; the theatre, I have a small part in a small theatre at the moment.

Any difficult moments? Not really. Oh yes, I could see that the waiter knew it was a blind date. That was embarrassing.

Good table manners? Very good. I like a girl who enjoys her food and she could use chopsticks. I was impressed with that.

Best thing about her? The green eyes! And she was really easy to talk to. She was interested and interesting. She didn't just talk about sport.

Did you go on somewhere? Well, we didn't go far. We found a piano – they are all over the city at the moment with signs saying 'Please play me'. I played, but I'm not very good. Sally sang, she can't sing at all. We made a terrible noise! It was good fun. Then she caught the bus home.

Marks out of 10? She can't sing, but I like her. 9

Would you like to meet again? Definitely. She left very hurriedly, but she has my number.

Vocabulary

7 Match the lines about Sally.

| Sally was interest**ed** | because she was funny and made him laugh. |
| Sally was interest**ing** | so she asked him a lot of questions. |

8 Complete the adjectives with *-ed* or *-ing*.

1 Thank you. That lesson was really interest_____ .

2 It's my birthday tomorrow so I'm very excit_____ .

3 Look at the view! It's amaz_____ .

4 I didn't like her new boyfriend. He was very bor_____ .

5 Don't be embarrass_____ . Everybody cries sometimes.

VOCABULARY
Right word, wrong word

Work with a partner. These exercises will help you think about how you learn new vocabulary. Use a dictionary.

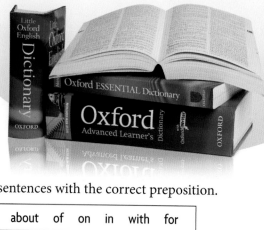

Verbs of similar meaning

1 Choose the correct verb for each line.

1 **play / go**

Can you _____ the piano?

Do you _____ running every morning?

2 **do / make**

I _____ too many mistakes in English.

I _____ my homework in the evening.

3 **speak / talk**

She can _____ three languages.

He can _____ forever! He never shuts up!

4 **say / tell**

Pardon! What did you _____ ?

Can you _____ me the time, please?

5 **pay for / buy**

How much did you _____ that meal?

Where can I _____ some sun cream?

Adjectives and nouns that go together

2 <u>Underline</u> two nouns that go with the adjective.

1 **important**	person / meeting / price
2 **delicious**	holiday / cake / meal
3 **high**	price / mountain / man
4 **long**	tree / journey / time
5 **heavy**	bag / sunshine / rain
6 **busy**	street / day / traffic

Prepositions

3 Complete the sentences with the correct preposition.

> to   from   at   about   of   on   in   with   for

1 He comes <u>from</u> Istanbul <u>in</u> Turkey.

2 He's crazy ___ football, but I'm not interested ___ it at all.

3 I am married ___ John. I met him ___ university ___ 2007.

4 I live ___ my parents ___ a flat ___ the first floor.

5 He's very good ___ playing the piano.

6 I like going ___ a walk ___ the park.

7 This is a photo ___ me ___ holiday ___ Spain.

8 I got this jumper ___ my sister ___ my birthday.

Words with two meanings

4 Look at these sentences. What are the two meanings of *date*?

> I met my husband on a blind **date**.
> **Dates** and raisins are good for you.

5 Write two sentences that show two possible meanings for these words.

left		
train		
run		
rest		
kind		
flat		
mean		

T 1.13 Listen to some sample answers.

EVERYDAY ENGLISH
Social expressions

1 In everyday situations we use a lot of social expressions. Read the expressions. Where are the people?

A 'Hi, Anna. How are you?'
B 'I'm fine, thanks. How are you?'

C 'Thank you so much.'
D 'My pleasure.'

E 'Can I help you?'
F 'No, thank you. I'm just looking.'

G 'Excuse me! Is that seat free?'
H 'No, sorry, I'm afraid it isn't.'

T 1.14 Listen and repeat. Pay attention to stress and intonation.

2 Match a line in **A** with a line in **B**.

A	B
1 Good morning!	___ Bye! See you later!
2 See you tomorrow!	___ Of course. What's the problem?
3 How do you do?	___ Never mind. Perhaps another time.
4 Thank you very much indeed.	___ Thanks! Same to you.
5 I'm sorry. I can't come tonight.	___ Good morning! Lovely day again.
6 Can you help me with this exercise?	___ Yeah! About 9.00, in the coffee bar.
7 Bye!	___ It doesn't matter. You're here now.
8 Bye! Have a good weekend.	___ Don't mention it. My pleasure.
9 Sorry I'm late.	___ How do you do? Pleased to meet you.
10 Cheers!	___ Cheers! Here's to your new job!

Bye! See you later!

Of course. What's the problem?

How do you do?

Good morning!

Thank you very much indeed.

T 1.15 Listen, check, and practise.

3 Choose a line to continue the conversations.
a I don't know what this word means.
b Yes, it's really warm for the time of year.
c Pleased to meet you, too.
d Thanks a lot. I'm excited, but a bit nervous.
e It was so kind of you!
f I'm free tomorrow night. What about that?
g Fine. 9.00 is good for me too.
h Yes. Let's meet after class.
i Thanks. Are you doing anything special?
j Yeah. I missed the bus.

T 1.16 Listen and check.

4 With a partner, choose two of the conversations. Continue them if you can and act them to the class.

> Good morning!

> Good morning! Lovely day again.

> Yes, it's really warm for the time of year.

> They say it's going to rain again tomorrow! Enjoy it while it lasts!

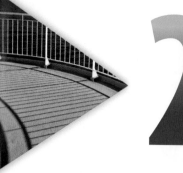

2 Whatever makes you happy

Present tenses • *have/have got* • Things I like doing • Making conversation

▷ STARTER

What is most important to you?
1 = most important, 6 = least important.

- ☐ good friends ☐ money
- ☐ a good job ☐ having fun
- ☐ being healthy ☐ family

Compare your ideas as a class.

For me, the most important thing is having a good job.

I LOVE WHAT I DO
Present tenses and *have/have got*

1 Look at the pictures of Ruth Flowers and Fraser Doherty. What's remarkable about them? Who likes going to clubs? Who makes jam?

2 **T 2.1** Read and listen to the article about Ruth. How old is she? What does she look like? What does her family think of her?

MAMY ROCK
the granny DJ

RUTH FLOWERS is not an ordinary grandmother. She's in her 70s, and has silver hair and bright-red lipstick. She's a DJ and works in clubs in Europe and tours festivals.

She lives alone in Bristol. She says, 'I've got a son and a grandson. They think what I'm doing is very cool!'

She likes rock bands such as Queen and the Rolling Stones, but she also plays electro and dance music. 'I love being with young people,' she says. 'They've got so much energy and enthusiasm!'

She's planning another European tour, and is currently making a new single.

'I'm having a lot of fun,' she says. 'I don't want it to stop.'

3 **T 2.2** Read and listen to the article about Fraser. What is his company? How old was he when he started it? What does his charity do?

the SuperJam
millionaire

FRASER DOHERTY is an extraordinary young man. He has his own company, SuperJam, which he started when he was just 16. 'I earn more money than my parents,' he says. His company makes jam – 500,000 jars every year – using a secret recipe from his grandmother.

All the major supermarkets sell his products. The business is growing fast – four flavours at the moment, but more on the way. And he has a charity that organizes huge tea parties for old people with live music and dancing.

'At the moment I'm very busy. I'm writing a cookbook. I've got an idea for a TV programme. And we're trying to get into the American market.'

GRAMMAR SPOT

1 Which two present tenses are used in the texts? Find examples of both.

2 Look at the sentences. Which refers to all time? Which refers to now?

He **makes** a lot of money.   He **has** his own company
She's **making** another single.   She's **having** a good time.

3 Find the examples of *have* and *have got* in the texts. Is *have got* more formal or informal? More spoken or written?

▶▶ **Grammar Reference 2.1 – 2.4 p74–75**

4 Work with a partner. Ask and answer questions about Ruth and Fraser.

RUTH	FRASER
1 What/do? **What does Ruth do? She's a DJ.**	1 What/do?
2 Where/work?	2 How much/earn?
3 How many children/have?	3 How many jars/ every year?
4 What sort of music/like?	4 Whose recipe/use?
5 Why/like young people?	5 What/writing?
6 What/doing at the moment?	6 What/trying to do?

T 2.3 Listen and check.

5 **T 2.4** Listen to an interview with Ruth. Does she like being famous? What do her friends think of her job? Complete the sentences.

1 I'm just an old lady _____ .

2 I _____ an old woman in an old people's home …

3 Because it _____ me happy!

4 It _____ how old you are.

6 **T 2.5** Listen to Fraser. What does he like about his work? What does he say about friends and family? Complete the interviewer's lines.

1 It _____ to me you really love what _____ !

2 _____ any free time?

3 _____ you _____ a girlfriend?

4 _____ you _____ much of your parents?

7 Ruth and Fraser both use the expression *'It's none of your/their business!'* What does this mean? What are they talking about?

PRACTICE

Talking about you

1 Look at the speech bubbles with *have* and *have got* in the question, negative, and short answer. How are the forms different?

T 2.6 Listen and practise.

> Do you have a car?
> Yes, I do.   No, I don't.
> Have you got a bike?
> Yes, I have.   No, I haven't.
> I don't have a camera.
> I haven't got an iPod.

2 Work with a partner. Ask and answer questions about these things.

- any pets
- a bike
- a laptop
- a camera
- an iPod
- a credit card
- any brothers and sisters
- the teacher /a big bag
- your parents /a holiday home

> Have you got any pets?
> What ...?
> Yes, I have.

Speaking – exchanging information

3 Look at the photos of Ilona, and Bill and Christina. With a partner, take turns to ask and answer questions about the people.

Student A Look at p83.
Student B Look at p84.

Ilona

> Where does Ilona come from?
> She comes from ...

Bill and Christina

> Where do Bill and Christina come from?
> They come from ...

State verbs

4 Some verbs don't usually take the Present Continuous. Complete the sentences with a verb in the Present Simple in the correct form.

think	not know	not believe	look	not agree	love
mean	not matter	need	own	not understand	

1 'What time is it?' 'I __don't know__ . Sorry.'
2 I'm thirsty! I _____ a drink.
3 I _____ your bag! Where did you get it?
4 'I _____ Thomas is stupid.'
   'I _____ . I think he's very clever.'
5 Her English isn't very good. I _____ her.
6 He's very rich. He _own_ a house in Mayfair.
7 You _look_ sad! What's the matter?
8 'Sorry I forgot your birthday!' 'Don't worry. It _doesn't_?'
9 'I'm 74 years old.'
   'I _don't bel_ you! You don't look a day over 60!'
10 I don't understand *learn by heart*. What _____ it _____ ?

Check it

5 Tick (✔) the correct sentence.

1 ☐ Angela live with her parents.
  ☐ Angela lives with her parents.

2 ☐ Where do you go on holiday?
  ☐ Where you go on holiday?

3 ☐ She doesn't work here anymore.
  ☐ She no works here anymore.

4 ☐ He's at the bus stop. He waits for a bus.
  ☐ He's at the bus stop. He's waiting for a bus.

5 ☐ I'm liking black coffee.
  ☐ I like black coffee.

6 ☐ I don't have got a phone.
  ☐ I haven't got a phone.

▶▶ **WRITING Writing a postcard** *p57*

VOCABULARY AND SPEAKING
Things I like doing

1 Work with a partner. Match a **Verb** and a **Phrase**.

Verb	Phrase
play	emails and texts
go out	games on my PlayStation
download	music and films
send	with my friends

Verb	Phrase
shop	in front of the TV
have	friends for a drink
relax	for clothes online
meet	a lie-in

Verb	Phrase
listen to	music
go out	nothing
get	for a meal
do	a takeaway pizza

Verb	Phrase
read	a football match live on TV
chat	to the gym
go	magazines
watch	to friends online

T 2.7 Listen, check, and practise.

2 When and where do you do some of these things?

> I like playing games on my PlayStation at home after school.

> I just love having a lie-in on Sunday mornings.

3 Complete the sentences with words from exercise 1.

1 I like shopping in the High Street, but mainly I ____shop online____ .

2 When I hear a band I like, I _____ their _____ from the Internet.

3 I _____ on my iPod when I go jogging.

4 I spend hours _____ , even though I'm with them all day at school!

5 Sometimes I like to chill out at home and _____ .

6 I'm always so tired after work I just want to _____ .

7 On Saturdays, I _____ , and don't get up till midday.

8 Do you want to cook tonight, or shall we _____ ?

9 It's Pete's birthday tonight, so we're _____ . Indian, I think.

10 I like keeping fit. I _____ three times a week.

T 2.8 Listen, check, and practise.

My perfect day

4 What is your idea of a perfect day? Make notes.

have a lie-in, go to a café, meet my friends

5 Work in groups. Talk about your perfect day.

> For me, a perfect day is when I have a lie-in, and go to a café for breakfast. Then, I meet my friends ...

READING AND SPEAKING
The happiness quiz

1 Look at the pictures. What are the people doing? Why are they happy?

2 Read the introduction to the quiz and answer the questions.

1 What does happiness depend on?
2 What do you need to know about yourself?
3 How can you learn to be happier?

3 Do the quiz and add up your score to see how happy you are. Do you agree?

4 The quiz is in four sections. Write one of these headings above each section.

Your enjoyment of life

Your health

Your relationships

Happiness with yourself

5 In which sections of the quiz did you score a high number? What do you need to do if you want to be happier?

What do you think?

6 Here are the results of a recent survey into happiness. Work in groups. Do you agree?

- £25,000 per year is all we need to make us happy.
- Buying things doesn't make us happy.
- Experiences such as holidays and living abroad *do* make us happier.
- Be happy with what you have. Stop wanting what you haven't got.
- Enjoy what you're doing.

7 **T 2.9** Listen to the beginning of the song, *Money*.

1 According to the song, what is more important, love or money?
2 'The best things in life are free.'
Does the singer agree? Do *you* agree?

Project

Research the life of someone rich and famous in the news at the moment. Has fame and fortune brought them happiness? Bring information and pictures to class. Tell the others about your person.

How happy are you?

Your happiness depends on how you see yourself, what you want from life, and how well you get on with other people.

But you need to know yourself. What sort of person are you? What makes you happy? Do you know how to make yourself happier? If you can answer these questions, you can learn to change the way you think and behave. And you *can* actually be happier. It just needs practice.

Do the quiz and find out how happy you are. Write 1–5 for each statement.

1 = very true   4 = not very true
2 = mainly true   5 = not true at all
3 = about 50/50

1 ☐ I take every opportunity to play, laugh, and have a good time.
2 ☐ I usually have a holiday at least once a year.
3 ☐ I get pleasure from lots of different things – art, nature, sport, friends …
4 ☐ Sometimes I get really enthusiastic about things.

5 ☐ I have the things in life that I think are important.
6 ☐ I have a positive image of myself.
7 ☐ I am grateful for what I have, and appreciate it.
8 ☐ I don't often feel jealous or envious of other people.

9 ☐ I sleep well and wake up feeling ready for a new day.
10 ☐ I keep fit and I take care of myself.
11 ☐ I never feel stressed when I have a lot of things to do.
12 ☐ I don't feel afraid or depressed.

13 ☐ I have close friends and people I share interests with.
14 ☐ I get a lot of satisfaction from my work/study.
15 ☐ My life makes a difference to other people.
16 ☐ I try to help other people.

☐ Add up your score

Your score – How happy are you?

16–28	Extremely happy
29–40	Happy enough
41–52	About average
53–64	Not very happy
65–80	Cheer up! Life can't be that bad!

LISTENING AND SPEAKING
Getting on with your neighbours

1 What do you know about your neighbours?

They're called ...   He's a ...   They've got ...   She's a ...

How well do you know them?

Really well/not at all/just to say hello to ...

2 What makes a good neighbour? Read the ideas.
Do you agree or disagree?

A good neighbour is someone who ...
- always says hello.
- doesn't make too much noise.
- I never see.
- minds his/her own business.
- invites me to parties.
- feels at home in my house.
- sometimes comes round for coffee.

Discuss your ideas in small groups.

Two neighbours

3 **T 2.10** You are going to listen to two neighbours,
Mrs Crumble and Alfie, talking about each other.
Read the questions.

First, listen to Mrs Crumble. Answer the questions.

1 Where is Alfie's flat?
2 Do Alfie and Mrs Crumble speak to each other?
3 What does he wear? What *doesn't* he wear?
4 Has he got a job?
5 What time does he go to bed? What time does he get up?
6 How many people are staying in Alfie's flat?
7 Has he got a girlfriend? Where does she live?
8 Why does he make such a noise? What's he doing now?
9 What does Alfie think of Mrs Crumble?

Check your answers in small groups.

4 **T 2.11** Now listen to Alfie. How does he answer questions
1–9. What differences are there?

5 In your groups, discuss who you think is telling the truth.

Roleplay

Work with a partner. Roleplay a conversation between Alfie
and Mrs Crumble where they actually get to know each other.

A Hello. I'm Alfie, your neighbour. You're Mrs Crumble,
   aren't you?
C Oh, Alfie, hello. I don't usually see you in the mornings ...

EVERYDAY ENGLISH
Making conversation

1 **T 2.12** It is the first day of a new school term. Listen to the conversations between two students and two teachers. The teachers are trying to be friendly. Which conversation is more successful? Why?

2 When you are having a conversation, it helps if you …
- add a comment
- don't just answer *yes* or *no*
- ask questions
- express interest

Find examples of these in **T 2.12** conversation 2 on p66.

1 John and Maria

3 Match a line in **A** with a reply in **B**.

A	B
1 What a lovely day it is today!	☐ a No, I didn't. I missed it.
2 Are you having a good time in London?	☐1 b Yes, beautiful, isn't it?
3 Have a good weekend!	☐ c Nothing special.
4 Did you have a nice weekend?	☐ d Thank you! They're new.
5 What are you doing tonight?	☐ e She's OK, thanks.
6 How's your mother these days?	☐ f Yes, I am. It's a very interesting city.
7 Did you watch the football last night?	☐ g Yes, I did. It was really good.
8 I like your shoes.	☐ h Thanks. Same to you.
9 If you have a problem, just ask me.	☐ i Thank you very much.

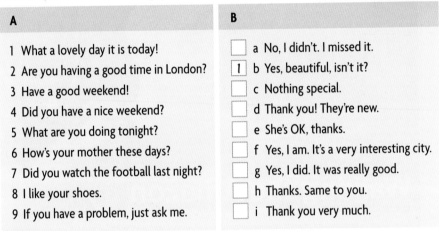

2 Maggie and Jean-Jacques

T 2.13 Listen and check. How does **B** keep the conversation going?

4 Practise the conversations with a partner. Cover **B**, then **A**. Remember the extra lines.

Keeping a conversation going

5 Work with a partner. Begin a conversation with one of these lines. Keep the conversation going as long as possible.

    ❝ I was on holiday last month. ❞

    ❝ I've got a new boyfriend/girlfriend. ❞

    ❝ I go to Hong Kong a lot on business. ❞

    ❝ I met the Queen yesterday. ❞

    ❝ I went shopping at the weekend. ❞

    ❝ Skiing is my favourite sport. ❞

T 2.14 Listen to an example and compare.

3 What's in the news?

Past Simple and Continuous • Adverbs • Saying when

1 What is the Past Simple of these verbs?
Which are regular? Which are irregular?

leave	take	become	begin
go	do	think	meet
walk	arrive	explain	end
want	decide		

2 Practise saying them around the class.

leave, left   *take, took*

HE WALKED 6,000 MILES!
Past Simple and Past Continuous

1 Look at Ed Stafford's web page. What was he the first to do?

2 Read and complete the text with verbs from the *Starter* in the Past Simple.

T 3.1 Listen and check.

3 Work with a partner. Write the questions.
  1 How far/Ed walk?
    How far did Ed walk?
  2 When/journey begin?
  3 Where/journey end?
  4 Which countries/go through?
  5 How long/journey take?
  6 Why/do it?

Now look at the map and read the text again. Answer the questions.

4 **T 3.2** Listen and check. Practise the questions and answers with your partner.

Walking the Amazon

Home | Map | Videos | Photos | Team | FAQs

Amazing journey ends after 6,000 miles

Ed Stafford ¹____*became*____ the first man in history to walk the length of the Amazon River from the source to the sea. He ²_____ for 860 days.

The journey ³_____ in April 2008 when Ed ⁴_____ the town of Camana on the Pacific coast of Peru. It ⁵_____ in August, 2010 when he ⁶_____ in Maruda, on the Atlantic coast of Brazil.

He ⁷_____ through three countries, Peru, Colombia, and Brazil. The journey ⁸_____ nearly two and a half years. 'I ⁹_____ it for the adventure,' says Ed.

Ed's journey

5 Read **Cho's story**. Who is Cho?

6 Which tense are the verbs in **bold** in Cho's story?
Complete these sentences.

1 Cho was working in the forest when he …
2 They were walking in a dangerous part of the forest when they …
3 The tribe didn't understand what Ed …

7 Write the questions. Ask and answer them with your partner.

1 What/Cho doing/when/met Ed?
2 Where/walking when/saw/tribe?
3 Why/tribe think/Ed/crazy?

T 3.3 Listen and check.

Cho's story

Home | Map | Videos | Photos | Team | FAQs

Ed didn't do the trip alone. His companion was Gadiel 'Cho' Sanchez Rivera, a forestry worker from Peru.

Cho said, 'When I first met Ed, I **was working** in the forest. I thought he was crazy, but I wanted to help him and be his guide.'

'One day we **were walking** in a very dangerous part of the forest when we saw a hostile tribe. They didn't understand what Ed **was doing** there. I explained he was an adventurer and he **was walking** the Amazon. They decided he was crazy, too.'

GRAMMAR SPOT

1 The Past Simple expresses a completed action in the past.
　　Ed **walked** the Amazon. He **began** his journey in 2008.

2 Complete the question and negative.
　　When _____ the journey begin?
　　They _____ finish the journey until 2010.

3 The Past Continuous expresses an activity in progress in the past.
　　Cho **was working** in the forest when he met Ed.

Compare these sentences.
　　I **had** a shower last night. (= simple, completed action)
　　I **was having** a shower when the phone rang. (= interrupted activity)

▶▶ **Grammar Reference 3.1–3.3 p76**　　▶▶ **Irregular verbs p87**

---

8 Read **Ed's blog**. Put the verb in brackets in the Past Simple or the Past Continuous.

Popular | Latest | Comments | Tags

Ed's blog

12 July
The day I nearly died

Today I ¹_____ (walk) next to the river when I nearly ²_____ (stand) on a snake. I ³_____ (stop) immediately. The snake's fangs ⁴_____ (go) in and out. I was terrified. I ⁵_____ (not move). One bite and you're dead in 3 hours.

10 September
Knives and guns!

Early this morning we ⁶_____ (cross) the river by boat when we ⁷_____ (see) five canoes. The tribesmen ⁸_____ (carry) knives and guns. They were angry because we ⁹_____ (not have) permission to be on their land. We ¹⁰_____ (leave) as fast as we could.

24 November
The jungle at night

I ¹¹_____ (lie) in my hammock last night trying to sleep, but it was impossible because the noise of the jungle was so loud. Monkeys ¹²_____ (scream) in the trees, and millions of mosquitos ¹³_____ (buzz) round my head. I ¹⁴_____ (take) a sleeping pill and finally ¹⁵_____ (fall) asleep at 3.00 a.m.

T 3.4 Listen and check.

9 Think of more questions to ask about Ed and Cho.

• What did they eat?　　• How did they navigate?

Go online and find out more about Ed. Were your questions answered? What else did you learn? Tell the class.

PRACTICE

Pronunciation

1 Write the past tense in the chart.

	/d/	/t/	/ɪd/
stop decide	stay**ed**	stopp**ed**	decid**ed**
stay work			
study play			
laugh phone			
want mend			
look answer			

T 3.5 Listen and check.

2 **T 3.6** Listen and repeat the sentences you hear.

We stayed in a hotel.   They stopped at lunch time.

3 **T 3.7** Listen and practise the sentences. Notice the pronunciation of *was* and *were*.

/wəz/
I was having dinner.

/wəz/
What was she wearing?

/wə/
They were playing football.

/wə/
Where were you going?

/wɒznt/
He wasn't listening.

/wɜːnt/
They weren't enjoying the party.

Discussing grammar

4 What's the difference between these pairs of sentences?

When we arrived, she **was making** some coffee.
When we arrived, she **made** some coffee.

I **read** a good book in bed last night.
I **was reading** a good book in bed last night.

5 Choose the correct verb form.

1 I *saw / was seeing* a good film yesterday.

2 While I *shopped / was shopping* this morning, I *lost / was losing* my wallet.

3 The police *stopped / were stopping* me on the motorway because I *drove / was driving* at 90 miles an hour.

4 'What *did you do / were you doing* when you saw the accident?'
'I *walked / was walking* down the street.'

5 'What *did you do / were you doing* when you saw the accident?'
'I *called / was calling* the police.'

6 'How *did you break / were you breaking* your leg?'
'I *was skiing / skied* and I *hit / was hitting* a tree.'

7 I *was cutting / cut* my finger while I *was cooking / cooked*.

8 *Did you have / Were you having* a good holiday?

Game – Truth or Lies

6 Write one true and two false sentences about where you were, and what you were doing at these times. Tell a partner.

- at 7.15 this morning
- at 1.00 p.m. yesterday
- at 10.00 p.m. last night
- at 10.00 a.m. last Sunday

Can your partner guess which sentence is true?

At 7.15 …

I was jogging in the park.

I was at home. I was getting ready for work.

I was coming home in a taxi after an all-night party.

Talking about the news

7 Look at these newspaper headings. What do you think the stories are about?

Texting woman falls into fountain

Chinese vase sells for £53 million

The app that saved an iPad

Granny stops robbery

Choose one of the stories. Read the article on page 85.

8 Work in small groups. Tell your story to the others. DON'T read it! The other students can ask questions.

LISTENING AND SPEAKING
The news

1 How do you keep up to date with what's happening in the world?

Which of these news topics interests you most?

> politics … celebrities … sport … fashion … culture … the arts …
> crime … international news … national news … local news …

Do you listen to the radio? Which station?

2 **T 3.8** Listen to five radio news headlines. What is the first story about? The second? Write a number 1–5.

- ☐ a strike
- ☐ a crime
- ☐ a death
- ☐ an explosion
- ☐ a football match

3 Which words do you think are from each story?

terrorists	thieves	guard	ex-wife
Picasso	cancer	goals	theft
half-time	higher pay	beat	protesting
injured	closed		

4 Write the question words.

_____ planted the bomb?

_____ paintings did they steal?

_____ are they on strike?

_____ times was he married?

_____ was the score?

Work in groups. Choose one of the news stories. What else do you want to know? Think of more questions. Write the questions on the board.

5 **T 3.9** Listen to the news stories. Which questions were answered?

Dictation

6 **T 3.10** You will hear the story about the art theft at dictation speed. One student should write the exact words on the board. The other students help.

> *That isn't how you spell thieves.*

> *You missed out a word.*

> *She didn't say that. She said . . .*

Project

7 Find a news story that interests you. Do some research. In the next lesson, bring in pictures and articles. Tell the class about the story. Be prepared to answer questions.

READING AND SPEAKING
The flight attendant who lost his cool

1 Talk as a class. What makes you lose your cool?

Bad drivers.   My little brother.

2 Look at the picture story about the flight attendant, Steven Slater. What made him lose his cool? In groups, write some sentences about the story. Compare ideas.

Aug 9 Flight from Pittsburgh arrives New York

EMERGENCY EXIT

3 Read each article. After each one, answer the questions and have a class discussion.

4 Look at the pictures in 2 again. Retell the story in more detail.

What do you think?

1 After August 16, this story 'died'. Why was it such big news for a week?

2 Steven Slater appeared in court two months later.
Do you think he paid a fine or went to prison?
Look at the article on p86 for the answer.
Do you think this was fair?

3 The artist Andy Warhol once said, 'In the future everyone will be famous for fifteen minutes'. How does the Steven Slater story illustrate this?

Steven Slater

1 10 August

Emergency exit for flight attendant who lost his cool

Flight attendant Steven Slater made an emergency exit from an Airbus after he had an argument with a passenger.

The incident happened at New York's JFK Airport soon after the JetBlue flight from Pittsburgh landed.

As the Airbus A320 was taxiing slowly on the runway, a passenger stood up to get her luggage. Mr Slater told her to sit down, but she refused. The businesswoman was taking her case out of the overhead locker when it hit Mr Slater on the head.

He started bleeding, and it was then that the flight attendant lost his temper. He marched to the front of the cabin and spoke furiously over the plane's PA system, saying, 'That's enough! After 28 years in this business, I quit!'

He then took two beers from a fridge, opened the door and activated the plane's emergency chute and jumped onto it. Mr Slater then ran to his car and drove home.

Police arrested Mr Slater at his home a short time later.

1 When and where did the incident happen?
2 What did the female passenger do?
3 What did the flight attendant say to her?
4 What did she do to him? How did he react?
5 How did Steven Slater leave the plane?

Discussion

• Was this a very important story?
• Why do you think it was in the newspapers?

2 | 11 August

Angry flight attendant becomes Facebook hero

The flight attendant Steven Slater, who left his plane via the emergency exit, is becoming a folk hero in the US.

Last night a 'Free Steven Slater' page on Facebook had 170,000 fans. People wrote how much they admired him. 'I would dearly love to quit my job like you did!' is the message from many.

Tens of thousands of people, including other cabin crew, left messages of support.

'You only did what everyone else feels like doing,' wrote one.

Slater appeared in court in New York yesterday and pleaded not guilty to charges of criminal damage and endangering life. He could face up to seven years in prison.

1 What did people think of Steven the next day?
2 How did they show their support?
3 Why did the public admire him?
4 What did other cabin crew say?

| Discussion |

• Why did people think he was a hero?

3 | 12 August

Steven Slater thanks public

Flight attendant Steven Slater, 39, who left his job after an attack by a passenger, said he was amazed by the public sympathy he received.

Slater has messages from millions of people all over the world.

He said, 'I really appreciate this enormous support.'

As he was leaving a Bronx police station, people were shouting 'You're a hero!' T-shirts that read FREE STEVEN SLATER are on sale.

JetBlue confirmed that Slater was still an employee, but suspended from duty.

1 How did Steven feel?
2 How did people show their support?
3 Where was he?

| Discussion |

• How is it possible that this story went round the world in two days?

4 | 15 August

Folk hero Slater relaxes on the beach

Ex-flight attendant Steven Slater spent the weekend relaxing on the beach. He was having a couple of beers and enjoying his new worldwide fame as the latest American folk hero.

The 39-year-old was wearing a grey T-shirt, white shorts, and a baseball cap as he talked to excited fans on the beach near his home in New York.

Yesterday supporters shouted, 'Good for you, Steve!' and 'We love you!' as he sat down on a chair, took off his shirt, and put on his sunglasses.

1 What is Steven called in the headline?
2 What actually happened on the beach?

| Discussion |

• Why was this day's story in the papers?
• What did Steven Slater do to deserve being called a folk hero?

5 | 16 August

Ex-flight attendant to get TV Show

Steven Slater is in talks to get his own reality show. TV production company Stone Entertainment wants to give the flight attendant the chance to star in a program that shows unhappy workers how to leave their job.

1 How is Steven going to become more famous?
2 What will the program be about?

| Discussion |

• Why did a TV production company want to give him a show?

JFK Airport

Folk hero

VOCABULARY
Adverbs

1 Look at these sentences from the articles on pages 26 and 27. Underline the adverbs.

> … he spoke furiously …

> … the Airbus A320 was taxiing slowly on the runway …

> 'I would dearly love to quit my job …'

2 Many regular adverbs end in *-ly*. Match a verb in **A** with an adverb in **B**.

A	B
1 drive	fluently
2 love	carefully
3 speak	patiently
4 rain	bravely
5 wait	heavily
6 fight	passionately

T 3.11 Listen and check. Try to remember the sentences.

3 What do you notice about the adjectives and adverbs in these sentences?

> Is this a **fast** train to London?
> Slow down! You drive too **fast**!

> I work **hard** and play **hard**.
> She's a very **hard** worker.

> I got up **late** this morning.
> We had a **late** breakfast.

4 What is the adverb from these adjectives? Complete the lines with the adverbs.

clear	quiet	slow	honest	perfect
complete	good	bad	easy	

1 play a game **well** and win
2 play a game … and lose
3 explain the rules …
4 shut the door …
5 forget something …
6 get out of bed …
7 play the piano …
8 pass an exam …
9 answer the questions …

Please
drive carefully
through our village

Word order

5 Correct the word order in these sentences.
1 She speaks very well English.
   She speaks English very well.
2 He started last week a new job.
3 Please read carefully the instructions.
4 Do you work still for the same company?
5 Never I can remember her name.
6 We had last year in Spain a holiday.

6 Put the adverbs in the correct place in the sentences.
1 My grandma is 75, and she goes swimming.
   (**nearly still regularly**)
2 'Do you love me?' 'I do. I'll love you.'
   (**really of course always**)
3 I was relaxing with a good book when someone knocked on the door. (**just really loudly**)
4 My sister is three, but she can read, and she can write.
   (**only already too**)
5 Break the eggs into a bowl with some milk and butter. Heat it gently. When it's ready, serve the scrambled eggs with toast. (**first then immediately**)
6 All my friends have a mobile phone. They're on Facebook. My dad's on Facebook. (**almost as well even**)

T 3.12 Listen and check.

▶▶ **WRITING** **T 3.13** Narrative writing *p58*

EVERYDAY ENGLISH
Saying when

1 Answer the questions. Tell a partner.
- What's the date today/tomorrow/the day after tomorrow?
- When's your birthday?
- What's your date of birth?
- What year were you born?

T 3.14 Listen and compare.

2 Look at the two ways of saying the date.

A What's the date today?	**A** What's the date today?
B It's the twenty-second of June.	**B** It's June the twenty-second.

Practise saying these dates in two ways.

T 3.15 Listen and check.

3 **T 3.16** Listen to how Americans say the dates. What's the difference between British and American English?

4 Practise saying the years.

2012 2002 2015
2010 1980 1969
1994 1848

5 **T 3.17** Write the dates you hear.

1 _____   3 _____   5 _____
2 _____   4 _____

6 What days are national holidays in your country?

7 Write down three dates that are important to you. Tell a partner.

July 25 – it's my wedding anniversary.

Time expressions

8 Complete the time expressions with *in/at/on*, or no preposition.

____ six o'clock	____ Saturday
____ 2004	____ Monday morning
____ last night	____ April
____ the weekend	____ yesterday evening
____ the evening	____ summer
____ January 18	____ two weeks ago
____ the 1960s	____ this morning
____ the other day	____ midnight

▶▶ **Grammar Reference 3.4 p76**

9 Work in small groups. When did you last …?
- go to the cinema

I went to the cinema last Friday/on Monday evening/ two weeks ago.

- play a sport
- go to a party
- do an exam
- have a holiday
- get a present
- buy some clothes
- go online
- cook a meal

4 Eat, drink, and be merry!

Expressing quantity • *something/no one …* • Articles • *A piece of …*
Can you come for dinner?

1 What did you eat and drink yesterday? Make a list.

2 Compare your list with the class.
   Who had the healthiest diet?

   For breakfast I had a cup of coffee, some cereal, and …

HOW TO LIVE TO BE 120!
Expressions of quantity

1 Read about Claus and Elvira Bonrich.
   1 What is their extraordinary ambition?
   2 What are their jobs?
   3 What kind of food do they eat? Do they cook any of their food?

An extraordinary ambition!

Claus Bonrich (33) and his wife **Elvira** (28) are a successful young couple. Claus is a software programmer and Elvira works in a health food shop. In many ways their life is quite ordinary, but they have an extraordinary ambition. They want to live until they are 120. And they believe they can do this by following an American health plan called the 'Calorie Restriction Diet'. Claus and Elvira eat a lot of raw food. They steam some food but they don't fry, grill, or roast anything, and there are many things they don't eat at all.

‘**We want to live to be 120!**’

2 Look at the nouns in the boxes. Which group can you count? Which can't you count? Label the nouns *Countable* and *Uncountable*.

_____	_____
apples grapes	meat fish
carrots prawns	orange juice coffee
vegetables calories	tea fruit
	broccoli alcohol

3 Work with a partner. Read and complete the questions and answers about the diet with the nouns from exercise 2.

1 Q Do you eat any ___meat___ ?
  A No, we don't eat **any** _____ at all, but we eat **some** _____ .

2 Q **How much** _____ do you eat?
  A We eat **a little** white _____ , but we love shellfish so we eat **a lot of** _____ .

3 Q Do you eat **much** _____ ?
  A Oh, yes, we eat **a lot of** fresh _____ – _____ and _____ , everything.

4 Q And do you eat **many** _____ ?
  A Yes, of course, we eat **lots of** raw _____ .

5 Q Don't you cook **any** vegetables at all?
  A We cook **some**. Sometimes we steam **a few** _____ and **a little** _____ .

6 Q And what do you drink?
  A Well, we don't drink **any** _____ or _____ , and naturally there's **no** _____ in our diet, but we do drink **a lot of** _____ .

7 Q **How many** _____ do you have every day?
  A About 1,500.
  A That's about 1,000 fewer than most people.

4 **T 4.1** Listen and check. Practise the questions and answers with your partner.

GRAMMAR SPOT

1 Look at the expressions of quantity in **A**, **B**, and **C**. Which group of expressions go with plural, count nouns? Which go with uncount nouns? Which go with both?

A	B	C
How much …?	How many …?	some/any
not much	not many	not any/no
a little	a few	a lot of/lots of

Find examples in the interview in exercise 3.

2 *Much* and *many* are not usually used in positive statements. When do we use them? Correct the sentences.

  There are ~~many~~ books in my bag. ✗
  There's ~~much~~ homework tonight. ✗

3 Look at these sentences. Which is a request?

  Is there *any* orange juice? Can I have *some* orange juice?

▶▶ **Grammar Reference 4.1 p77**

5 Work in small groups. Do you think the Bonrichs eat and drink the things in the box? Discuss with your partner and complete the lists.

~~cereal~~	~~bread~~	milk	cheese	butter
tomatoes	peppers	olive oil	nuts	rice
pasta	sugar	bananas	mangoes	biscuits
apple juice	potatoes	chips	crisps	wine
tap water	mineral water			

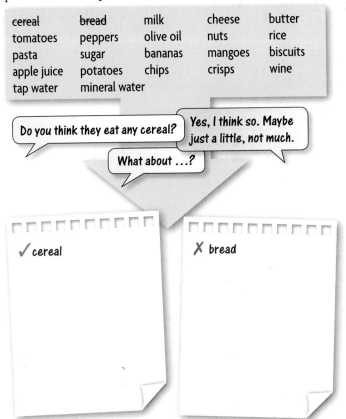

Do you think they eat any cereal?

Yes, I think so. Maybe just a little, not much.

What about …?

✓ cereal

✗ bread

Compare your list with the class.

6 **T 4.2** Listen and find out if your ideas were correct.

7 What do you think of the diet? Will the Bonrichs live to be 120? Why/Why not?

PRACTICE

Discussing grammar

Work with a partner. Complete the sentences.

1 some / any

1 Have they got _____ children?
2 We don't need _____ olive oil.
3 Can you lend me _____ money?
4 Is there _____ petrol in the car?
5 Can I have _____ cake?

2 much / many

1 Have you got _____ homework?
2 We don't need _____ eggs. Just half a dozen.
3 Is there _____ traffic in your town?
4 I don't know _____ students in this class.
5 How _____ time have you got?

3 a little / a few / a lot of

1 I have _____ very close friends. Two or three.
2 He has _____ money. He's a millionaire.
3 'Do you take sugar in coffee?' 'Just _____. Half a spoonful.'
4 I'll be ready in _____ minutes.
5 She speaks good Spanish, but only _____ Russian.

something/someone/somewhere ...

4 Complete the lines with the correct word.

some any		thing one/body
every no	**+**	where

1 'Did you meet _____ nice at the party?'
  'Yes. I met _____ who knows you!'
2 'Ouch! There's _____ in my eye!'
  'Let me look. No, I can't see _____?'
3 'Let's go _____ hot for our holidays.'
  'But we can't go _____ that's too expensive.'
4 'Where are my glasses? I can't find them _____?'
  'What are they on the top of your head?'
5 'It was a great party. _____ loved it.'
  'They did. _____ wanted to go home.'
6 'Did you get _____ nice in the sales?'
  'No, _____. I couldn't find _____ I liked.'

T 4.3 Listen and check. Practise them with a partner.

5 **T 4.4** Listen. There is a word missing in each sentence. Call out what it is. Say the complete sentence.

> Do you know ... famous?
>
> ANYONE!

32 Unit 4 • Eat, drink, and be merry!

THE SECRET TO A LONG LIFE
Articles – a/an, the

1 Do you know anybody who lived to be a great age? How old were they? Why do you think they lived so long?

2 **T 4.5** Read and listen to the text. Answer the questions.

1 How long did the grandfather live?
2 Where did he live?
3 What kind of shop did he have?
4 How many children did he have?
5 Why did everybody love him?
6 When did he stop work?
7 What was his secret to a long life?

My Grandfather's

My grandfather lived until he was **101** years old. He was a shopkeeper. He had a fish and chip shop in an old village near a big, industrial town in the north of England. He had a son and a daughter. The daughter is my mother. The family lived above the shop.

In those days, fish and chips was the most popular dish in the whole country. My grandfather made the best fish and chips in the area. People came to the village – by bus especially to get them.

Everybody loved my grandfather because he was such a happy and contented man. He worked hard, but once a week he closed the shop and went to have lunch (not fish and chips!) with friends in the local pub. He didn't retire until he was 78 years old. He said that the secret to a long life was a glass of whisky before going to bed and lots of fish and chips.

GRAMMAR SPOT

Articles

1 Find examples of the definite article (*the*) and the indefinite article (*a/an*) in the text.

2 What do you notice about these phrases?

> ...came **by bus**.
> ...went to **have lunch**.
> ...before going **to bed**.

3 Read the rules in **Grammar Reference 4.2 p77**. Find some examples of these rules in the text.

Reading aloud

1 Join the lines about the grandfather with *the*, *a*, *an*, or no article.

My grandfather was		shopkeeper.
He lived in		north of England.
He had a fish and chip shop in		old village.
His family lived above	**the**	shop.
He made	**a**	best fish and chips in the area.
Some people came by	**an** **no article**	bus to the shop.
He closed the shop once		week.
He went to have		lunch with friends.
He liked to have		little whisky before bed.

T 4.6 Listen and check. Read the lines aloud to a partner.

Discussing grammar

Work with a partner.

2 Complete the sentences with *a/an*, *the* or no article.

1 He has _____ boy and _____ girl. _____ boy is 22 and _____ girl is 17.

2 His son is _____ engineer and his daughter is _____ student.

3 He always has _____ cheese sandwiches for _____ lunch.

4 All _____ family stayed at _____ Grand Hotel.

5 _____ few people came by _____ taxi to _____ party.

6 It was such _____ wonderful party. We had _____ best time ever.

7 I don't go out to _____ work. I work at _____ home on my computer.

8 I do all my shopping on _____ Internet. What _____ great way to shop!

Check it

3 Find one mistake in each sentence and correct it.

1 He's postman, so he has breakfast at 4.00 a.m.

2 The love is more important than money.

3 I come to school by the bike.

4 I'm reading one good book at the moment.

5 'Where are the children?' 'In a kitchen.'

6 I live in centre of town, near the hospital.

7 My parents bought the lovely house in the country.

8 I don't eat the bread because I don't like it.

READING AND LISTENING
Unusual places to eat

1 Are there lots of places to eat and drink in your town? What are they? Where did people in your country eat and drink hundreds of years ago?

2 Read the introduction. Look at the pictures and the Fact Files. What's unusual about the three restaurants?

3 Work in three groups.

> **Group A** Read about *Dinner in the Sky*.
>
> **Group B** Read about *Ithaa Undersea Restaurant*.
>
> **Group C** Read about *'s Baggers Restaurant*.

Answer the questions about your restaurant.
1 Where is the restaurant?
2 In what ways is it unusual?
3 When did it open?
4 What's on the menu? Is it good?
5 How expensive is it?
6 Are there any problems?

4 Find a partner from the other two groups and compare the restaurants.

Listening

5 **T 4.7** Listen to people who visited the restaurants. Answer these questions after each person.

- Which restaurant did they visit? Who with?
- What was good about it?
- What wasn't so good?
- What do they say about the other guests?

Alexander	Hans	Lucy

What do you think?

- Which do you think is the *most* unusual restaurant?
- Which would you like to visit? Why?
- Do you eat out? How often? What's your favourite resturant?
- Do you know any unusual restaurants? Tell the class.

No ordinary
place to eat!

Dinner in the Sky

FACT FILE
- 50m up in the air
- a table 9m x 5m
- diners hang from a crane
- there isn't a loo

Dinner in the Sky is for people who want more than a little excitement when they go out to eat. They sit at a huge table which hangs from a crane fifty metres in the air. It's not a good idea for people who are afraid of heights or for those who don't have much money. It costs £10,000. The twenty-two diners wear seat belts and relax and enjoy the views while the chefs prepare the finest food in front of them. The restaurant opened in Belgium in 2006, but now has branches in Paris, Dubai, Florida, and Las Vegas.

David Ghysels, the Belgian organizer says, 'We realized that people were bored with going to the same old restaurants. They wanted to try something different. The sky's the limit with us!'

The crane is checked carefully before every sitting. The table is 9m x 5m and weighs six tonnes. In the centre there is a sunken platform for the chef and two waiters. The food is delicious, but most guests don't feel like eating until after a few drinks! Then they also get the courage to look down at the ground where tiny people are looking up in amazement and waving.

Dinner in the Sky is very exciting and the food is good, but there are problems. For example, even in quiet weather conversation is difficult because of the wind. Guests shout to each other across the table. Also, the loo. You can't go to the loo until the table descends again. Difficult for some! But later, back on earth, after a visit to the loo, the guests have a great experience to talk about.

For hundreds of years when tired travellers stopped on their journeys, there were only a few places to eat and drink. Nowadays, streets are lined with restaurants, cafés, and snack bars, but some people want something more unusual.

Ithaa Undersea Restaurant

FACT FILE
- 5m under the sea
- a huge glass ceiling
- diners wear formal clothes
- they eat face-to-face with sharks

Welcome to the Maldives and the first underwater restaurant in the world. The *Ithaa Undersea Restaurant* on Rangali Island sits five metres below the Indian Ocean. Ithaa means 'pearl' in the Maldivian language and the guests are like pearls in a glass oyster.

It's not cheap – about £160 for dinner – and there aren't many seats, only a dozen, so it's not easy to get a reservation even if you've got enough money. However, it is easy to get to. You don't need to be a swimmer or a scuba diver, but you do have to wear formal clothes. You simply descend to the restaurant down some spiral stairs.

The manager, Carlton Schieck says, 'We have used aquarium technology to put diners face-to-face with the fish. Our guests are speechless at the colour and beauty of the underwater world. They can enjoy the views and the fine food and not get their feet wet.'

The views are spectacular. In the crystal-blue sea, a few metres from your head, there are sharks, sting rays, turtles, and thousands of tropical fish looking at you as you eat. There is also a fabulous coral garden to add to the colour. The experience is both romantic and magical – and you can guess what's on the menu!

The restaurant opened in 2004 and cost over £3 million to build. In April 2010 it also became a hotel. If you want more excitement and would like to sleep underwater with the fish, you can do this for just £7,500 a night!

However, an underwater building can't last forever. It is thought that it will have a life of about twenty years.

's Baggers Restaurant

FACT FILE
- no waiters
- food lands from above
- email as you eat
- eat now, pay later
- no tips

Germany likes to call itself *The Land of Ideas* and *'s Baggers Restaurant* in Nuremberg is certainly an amazing idea. It's a restaurant with no waiters to serve you. You do everything for yourself with touch-screen TVs and computers. It opened in 2007 and is the first automated restaurant in the world.

When you arrive you pick up an *'s Baggers* credit card and go to sit at a big, round table with three or four computer screens. You put your card into the computer and order your meal by touching the pictures on the screen. You don't see the chefs. They are in the kitchen high above you. They're real men, not machines (at least not yet). The food is all freshly cooked and when it is ready it is put in a pot and sent down a spiral tube where it lands on the table in front of you. This gives a new meaning to fast food! The TVs are connected to the Internet, so if you get bored while waiting, you can send and receive emails and text messages.

A businessman called Michael Mack had the idea for *'s Baggers*. He decided that waiters were unnecessary and too expensive. 'You don't need waiters to run to and from customers taking orders to the kitchen and back.' Mack is planning to open more restaurants and now has the patent for the idea.

The meals are not too expensive – about €8 (£6) a portion. And if you want you can pay by direct debit at the end of the month. And something else that saves money – there is, of course, no need to leave a tip!

VOCABULARY AND LISTENING
A piece of …

1 Work in small groups. Match amounts in **A** with nouns in **B**. How many can you make?

A		B
a piece a loaf a bottle a can a kilo a litre a packet a pair a slice a bunch	**of**	apples bananas beer bread cake chewing gum Coke flowers ham tissues jeans milk paper petrol sunglasses socks wine

2 **T 4.8** Listen and repeat the expressions. How much are some of these things in your country?

I think a large loaf of white bread costs about £1.00.

3 **T 4.9** Listen to six conversations.

1 Where is the conversation taking place? Choose from these places.
- a newsagent's
- a clothes shop
- a chemist's
- an off-licence
- a café
- a supermarket

2 What does the customer want to buy?
3 What numbers and/or prices do you hear? Write them down.

4 Who says these lines? What is each line about?

1 'No problem. I've got change.'
2 'Have you got any in blue?'
3 'I'm afraid there are only two slices left.'
4 'Take these three times a day.'
5 'Have you got any ID?'
6 'They're on the first aisle, over there.'

5 **T 4.9** Listen again and check. Work with a partner. Turn to page 69 and choose one of the conversations. Learn it by heart and then act it to the class.

▶▶ **WRITING** Writing an email *p60*

EVERYDAY ENGLISH
Can you come for dinner?

1 What is happening in the picture? What are the people eating and drinking?

2 Match a question in **A** with a response in **B**.

A
1 Would you like some more rice?
2 Could you pass the salt, please?
3 Can I have some water, please?
4 Please, just help yourselves to the dessert.
5 Would anybody like some more ice cream?
6 How would you like your coffee?
7 This is delicious! Would you mind giving me the recipe?
8 Do you want some help with the washing-up?

B
____ a Black, no sugar. Have you got any decaf?
____ b No, not at all. I got it online. I'll give you the website.
____ c Do you want still or sparkling?
____ d No, thanks. But could I have another piece of bread?
____ e Yes, of course. Do you want the pepper, too?
____ f No, but I'd love some more fruit. Is there any left?
____ g No, of course not. You're our guests!
____ h We will. It looks fantastic. Did you make it yourself?

T 4.10 Listen and check. What is the next line? Practise the conversations with a partner.

3 Complete the requests with *Can/Could I ...?* or *Can/Could you ...?*

1 _____ have some apple juice, please?
2 _____ tell me where Market Street is, please?
3 _____ see the menu, please?
4 _____ use your iPad for a few minutes, please?
5 _____ lend me £20, please?
6 _____ take me to school, please?
7 _____ help me with my homework, please?
8 _____ give me a lift to the station, please?

Practise the requests with a partner. Give an answer for each request.

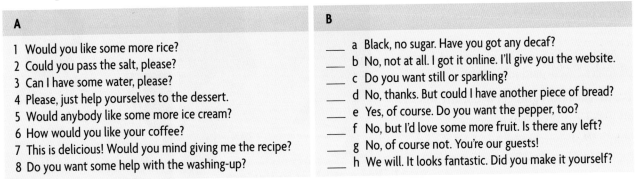

Can I have some apple juice, please?

Sorry, we ...

Yes, of course. Would you like ...?

T 4.11 Listen and compare.

4 Make 5–8 in exercise 3 more polite using *Would you mind + -ing*?

Would you mind lending me £20?

No, not at all. Is 20 enough?

T 4.12 Listen and check. Practise saying them.

5 Request things from your teacher and other members of the class.

Can I borrow your ...?

Could you lend me your ...?

Would you mind helping me with ...?

5 Looking forward

Verb patterns • Future forms • Phrasal verbs • Expressing doubt and certainty

▶ **STARTER**

Complete these sentences with ideas about you. Tell the class.

- *One day I want to …*
- *Tonight I'm …*
- *Right now, I'd like to …*
- *This weekend I'm going to …*

I'D LIKE TO …
Verb patterns

1 Read what the people say. What do they do? What are their problems? What do you think they want to do?

2 Work with a partner. Which sentences go with which person.

> 1 'I'm going to study hard for my exams because I hope to get a well-paid job.' **Abby**
>
> 2 'I'd like to leave now and get a job, any job. I want to earn some money.'
>
> 3 'I'm thinking of applying for another job with a company in New York.'
>
> 4 'Now I like sleeping late and planning holidays on the Internet for me and my wife.'
>
> 5 'I'm looking forward to having a good break. We're going to Spain this summer.'
>
> 6 'I enjoy looking after the kids, but I'd love to travel, too.'

T 5.1 Listen and check. What else does each person say?

3 **T 5.1** Listen again. Complete the lines. Who says them?

1 I'd love __to work__ there for a couple of years.
2 I'm planning _____ nothing but read on the beach.
3 I _____ owing so much money.
4 I get fed up with _____ at home all day. I'm looking forward to _____ back to work.
5 I'm pretty good at _____ a computer.
6 My mum and dad say that I _____ leave school.

TOM

I'm 16 and I'm fed up with school and exams …

ABBY

I'm a student in my last year at university. I've got debts of nearly £25,000 …

KELLY

I'm a paramedic. I love my job but it's very stressful …

ALISON

I've got three kids under seven and my husband works abroad a lot of the time …

GRAMMAR SPOT

1 Find examples in exercises 2 and 3 of:

verb + infinitive   verb + *-ing*

prepositions *at, of, with* and *to + -ing*

2 What's the difference between these sentences?

I **like working** in New York.

I'**d like to work** in New York.

3 Complete the sentences with the phrase *work in New York*. Put the verb *work* in the correct form.

I want …   *to work in New York.*

I'd love …

I enjoy …

I'm fed up with …

I hope …

I'm thinking of …

I'm looking forward to …

▶▶ **Grammar Reference 5.1 p78**   ▶▶ **Verb patterns p87**

MARTIN

I work in IT. There's nothing I don't know about computers but I need a change …

BILL

I'm a retired newsagent and I didn't have a day off for 40 years …

Discussing grammar

1 In these sentences, one or two verbs are correct, but not all three. Work with a partner. Tick (✓) the correct verbs.

1 I ___ to work in Paris.
   a ✓ want   b ☐ enjoy   c ✓ 'd like

2 We ___ going to Italy for our holidays.
   a ☐ are hoping   b ☐ like   c ☐ 're thinking of

3 She ___ leave work early tonight.
   a ☐ wants   b ☐ 'd like   c ☐ can't

4 I ___ to see you again soon.
   a ☐ hope   b ☐ 'd like   c ☐ 'm looking forward

5 He ___ playing sports games on the Wii.
   a ☐ wants   b ☐ 's good at   c ☐ enjoys

6 Are you ___ learning foreign languages?
   a ☐ want   b ☐ like   c ☐ good at

7 We ___ having a few days off soon.
   a ☐ 're going   b ☐ 'd love   c ☐ 're looking forward to

8 I ___ doing housework.
   a ☐ 'm fed up with   b ☐ hate   c ☐ don't want

T 5.2 Listen and check.

2 Make sentences with the verbs which *weren't* correct in exercise 1. Read them aloud.

T 5.3 Listen and check.

> I enjoy working in Paris.

Making questions

3 Write the questions.

1 I hope to go to university. (*What/want/study?*)
2 One of my favourite hobbies is cooking. (*What/like/make?*)
3 I'm bored. (*What would/like/do?*)
4 I'm looking forward to the party. (*Who/hoping/see/there?*)
5 We're planning our summer holidays. (*Where/think/go?*)

T 5.4 Listen and check. How do the conversations continue? Practise some of them with a partner.

Talking about you

4 Ask and answer the questions with a partner.

- Where would you like to be right now?
- Do you like learning English?
- Would you like to learn any other languages? Which?
- Would you like to have a break now?

▶▶ **WRITING** **T 5.5** **Writing for talking** *p61*

HAVE YOU GOT ANY PLANS?

will, *going to*, and Present Continuous for future

1 Match questions 1–4 with an answer from Pete and an answer from Debbie. Who has got definite future plans? Who hasn't?

> 1 What are you doing this evening?
> 2 Are you doing anything interesting this weekend?
> 3 Are you going to have a party for your birthday?
> 4 Where are you going on holiday?

Pete

a Of course! I'm going to invite all my friends.

b I'm going surfing for two weeks in Costa Rica.

c Yes, I am. I'm going to stay with an old school friend.

d I'm meeting my brother for a drink.

Debbie

e I haven't thought about it. Maybe I'll just celebrate at home with a few friends.

f I can't decide. Perhaps I'll go cycling in France.

g No, I'm not. I'll give you a ring and maybe we can do something together.

h Nothing much. I think I'll just watch a DVD and order a pizza.

T 5.6 Listen and check.

2 Pete is talking to his friend, Ben. Debbie is talking to Ella. Answer the questions.

1 Why can't Ben go out with Pete and his brother?
2 Why is Pete going to visit his old school friend?
3 Where's Ben going on holiday?
4 Where's Ella going on holiday?
5 When's Debbie's birthday?
6 Why won't Ella stay late?

Talking about you

3 With your partner ask and answer the four questions in exercise 1 about you.

GRAMMAR SPOT

Will, *going to* and the Present Continuous can all refer to future time.

1 **Will** can express an intention decided *at* the time of speaking.

   I'll give you a ring.

2 **Going to** can express a plan decided *before* the time of speaking.

   I'm going to stay with a friend.

3 The **Present Continuous** can express an arrangement.

   I'm working late this evening.

▶▶ **Grammar Reference 5.2 p78**

PRACTICE

Discussing grammar

1 Work with a partner. Choose the correct verb form.

1 A Have you decided which university to apply for?
   B Oh yes, *I'll* / *I'm going to* apply for Oxford.

2 A I haven't got your mobile number.
   B Really? *I'll* / *I'm going to* text it to you right now.

3 A We don't have any fruit in the house.
   B *I'll go* / *I'm going* shopping this afternoon.
   I'll / *I'm going to* get some apples.

4 A My bag is really heavy.
   B Give it to me. *I'll* / *I'm going to* carry it for you.

5 A Tony's back from holiday.
   B Is he? *I'll* / *I'm going to* give him a ring.

6 A What *will we have* / *are we having* for supper?
   B *I'm going to* / *I'll* make spaghetti bolognese.

T 5.7 Listen, check, and practise. What's the extra line?

What can you say?

2 [T 5.8] Close your books. Listen to the first line of six conversations. Respond to each one.

> Why are you looking forward to the weekend?

> Because I'm going to the theatre …

3 [T 5.9] Listen and compare.

When can we meet?

4 Work with a partner. Arrange a time to meet in the next week.
Student A Look at your diary on p83.
Student B Look at your diary on p84.

> What are you doing on Monday afternoon?

> I'm …

Will you, won't you?

5 Use the words in **A** and make sentences with *I think … will …*. Match them with a line in **B**.

> I think you'll pass your driving test. You won't fail again.

A

1 you/pass your driving test
2 my team/win
3 it/warm today
4 I/join a gym
5 they/get divorced
6 I/go by train

B

___ I won't go on a diet.
___ You won't fail again.
___ You won't need your jumper.
___ I won't fly.
___ They won't stay together.
___ They won't lose this time.

6 [T 5.10] Listen and check. What is the extra line?

LISTENING AND SPEAKING
How does it feel to be 20-something?

1 Think of someone you know in their twenties. Tell a partner about them.
name • age • relationship to you • job • interests • ambitions

2 *The Times* newspaper ran an 'iGeneration' poll to find out how it feels to be a 20-something in the 21st century. What is a 20-something?

3 [T 5.11] Listen to three 20-somethings, Leo, Elsa, and Dan. Who is happy? Who feels grown-up? Who knows what they want to do in the future?

I still can't believe I'm a grown-up!

Leo 28   Elsa 26   Dan 24

4 Complete the questions with the correct name.

1 How old is __Leo__'s nephew?
2 How much did _____ owe when he left university?
3 Why did _____ give up studying law?
4 How much does _____ earn as a junior reporter?
5 How long did _____ go travelling?
6 What questions did _____'s nephew ask?

Ask and answer the questions with a partner.

5 [T 5.11] Listen again. After each 20-something, answer the questions.

Leo
1 Why was he shocked by his nephew's questions?
2 Why is he happy?
3 What's he going to do next year?
4 When does he think he'll marry?

Elsa
5 Where did she go travelling?
6 What is she doing at the moment?
7 What question does her father ask?
8 How is her life different from her mother's at the same age?

Dan
9 Why is he a *boomerang kid*?
10 Does he think that his situation is unusual?
11 When does he think he'll marry his girlfriend?
12 Why is he fed up?

What do you think?
• When do you think is the best time for children to leave home?
• What are the pros and cons for parents if their children move back home?
• What are the pros and cons for the children?

READING AND SPEAKING
Hope for the future

1 Do you know the name Chernobyl? Do you know where it is? Find out about it on the Internet. Discuss with the class.

2 Read the introduction to Palina – the girl with two families.
- Where does Palina come from?
- Why didn't her future look good?
- When was she born?

3 Read Life in the village of Polessye. Are the sentences true (✓) or false (✗)? Correct the false ones.

1 Palina was born the same year as the disaster.
2 She grew up on a farm.
3 She was an only child.
4 Eight experts from Minsk came to her school.
5 There was a forest near the village.
6 The experts paid for the children to have holidays abroad.
7 Palina wanted to go to Ireland because she could speak English.

4 Read Life in Ireland. Answer the questions.

1 How did Palina communicate with the family?
2 Why was she so surprised in the shopping mall?
3 Was her English fluent at the end of the holiday?
4 How often did she visit the Irish family?

5 Read Palina today. Why is Palina lucky? What reasons can you find?

6 Read the sentences. Who do you think said each one?

1 'It's difficult to sell any of our produce these days.'
2 'We aren't going to pick any more mushrooms.'
3 'Would you like to have a holiday in Ireland?'
4 'I'm a bit worried about going.'
5 'Welcome to Ireland. We hope you'll be happy here.'
6 'Let's play in the garden!'
7 'We'll pay for your education.'
8 'One day I'm going to return as a doctor.'

What do you think?
- 'The disaster changed the lives of everybody in the village.' How do you think life changed?
- What do you learn about Palina and her family that suggests that they were poor?
- Do you think Palina was ever homesick?

Roleplay

Work in groups and think of questions to ask Palina about her life. In pairs take the roles of Palina and the interviewer. Ask and answer questions, begin like this.

Nice to meet you Palina. Can I ask you some questions?

Of course.

When and where were you born?

T 5.12 Listen and compare.

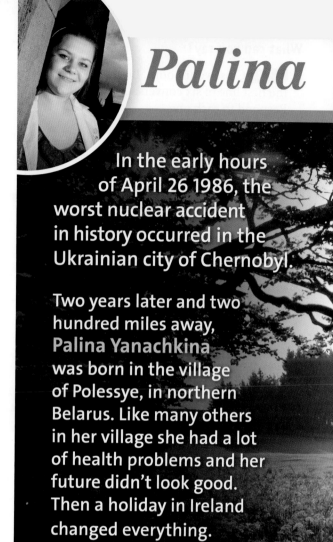

Palina

In the early hours of April 26 1986, the worst nuclear accident in history occurred in the Ukrainian city of Chernobyl.

Two years later and two hundred miles away, Palina Yanachkina was born in the village of Polessye, in northern Belarus. Like many others in her village she had a lot of health problems and her future didn't look good. Then a holiday in Ireland changed everything.

– the girl with two families

The Yanachkina family

Life in the village of Polessye

The nuclear disaster changed the lives of everybody in the village. It took away all hope for the future. However, when Palina was born in 1988 her parents did their best to give her and her brother Micha a good life. They were farmers and before the accident, sold meat, fruit, and vegetables to the international market. After the disaster, no one wanted to buy anything.

The villagers were often ill and depressed. When Palina was eight, experts from the capital, Minsk, came to her school and did health tests on the children. The experts told them to stop picking the mushrooms in the forest because they were badly contaminated. When she was ten the experts returned with news of a charity that helped children like her have holidays abroad. They asked Palina if she would like to go to Ireland and stay with a family in Limerick. Palina felt a bit nervous about leaving home and she didn't speak a word of English, but she decided to go.

The Quaid family

Life in Ireland

When Palina met her Irish family, she liked them immediately. John and Fiona Quaid and their two children, Chloe, three, and Evan, six, gave Palina a warm welcome. At first the only way to communicate was with a phrase book, but soon she became good friends with the children. They didn't need language to play.

So many things in Ireland surprised Palina. They visited a shopping mall and she couldn't believe her eyes, there was so much to choose from. She only knew her little village shop. She missed her family, but couldn't speak to them because they didn't have a phone.

By the time she went home, Palina could speak a few words of English and was delighted when the Quaids invited her back for Christmas. After that she started to visit the family twice a year and often spent three months with them in summer.

Palina today: 'I'm so lucky!'

When Palina was in her teens the experts returned to Polessye and checked her again. They couldn't believe how healthy she was. Her time in Ireland was improving her health and her English.

In her free time Palina helped run the farm. However, she didn't want to continue doing this for the rest of her life. She dreamed of becoming a doctor, but had no money to study. John and Fiona understood her problem. They offered to pay for her to study in Ireland and said she could stay with them full-time. Palina was amazed and delighted. It was hard for her parents, but they wanted the best for their daughter.

Palina is now studying biochemistry at the University of Limerick. She hopes to study medicine one day and return to Belarus to help those who are not as lucky as she is.

VOCABULARY AND SPEAKING
Phrasal verbs – literal

Phrasal verbs consist of a verb + adverb/preposition. Some phrasal verbs are literal. Look at these examples.

> I wanted to **move back** home. (move + back)
> It **took away** all hope for the future. (take + away)
> She **grew up** in a small village. (grow + up)

1 Complete the sentences with a word from the box.

> out   at   down   on   back   off

1 Come in and take _____ your coat!
2 **Put** _____ something warm. It's cold today.
3 There's some ice cream in the freezer. Can you **get** it _____?
4 If you don't feel well, go and **lie** _____.
5 **Look** _____ the countryside. Isn't it beautiful?
6 I'll lend you £20. **Pay** me _____ when you can.

2 Work with a partner. Take turns to mime one of these phrasal verbs. Can you guess what your partner is doing?

- throw something away
- try something on
- look for something
- turn something off
- turn round
- pick something up

3 Complete the sentences with a phrasal verb from exercise 2. Read them aloud.

1 I'm _____ my glasses. I can't find them anywhere.
2 I like these jeans. Can I _____ them _____?
3 Those jeans look great. _____ _____ so I can see the back!
4 Don't drop litter on the floor! _____ it _____!
5 Don't _____ _____ that newspaper. I want to read it.
6 Why are all these lights on? _____ them _____.

Phrasal verbs – idiomatic

Some phrasal verbs are idiomatic.

> I **gave up** my job because I was bored. (= stopped)
> She **picked up** English from the children. (= learnt bit by bit)
> The plane **took off** late. (= left the ground)

4 Match the phrases with the pictures.

> look up a word   look after a baby   run out of milk
> fall out with someone   get on well with somebody

5 Complete the sentences with a phrasal verb from exercise 4. Read them aloud.

1 'What does this word mean?' 'I don't know. I'll _____ it _____.'
2 My boss is a great guy. I _____ very well _____ him.
3 Leave little Emma with me. I'll _____ her while you're out.
4 It was a terrible journey – traffic jams all the way, and we nearly _____ petrol.
5 I feel miserable because I _____ my best friend at the weekend.

Talking about you

Complete the questions with one of the phrasal verbs on this page in the correct form.

1 Where did you _____? Do you still live in the same house?
2 How do you _____ your parents?
3 Do you ever _____ your friends and stop speaking to them?
4 Would you like to be a doctor or nurse and _____ people?
5 Are you good at _____ foreign languages?
6 Do you _____ lots of words in your dictionary?

T 5.13 Listen and check. Ask and answer the questions about you with a partner.

EVERYDAY ENGLISH
Expressing doubt and certainty

1 Read the questions and the possible answers. Which are …?

- 100% certain
- 75% certain
- 50% certain

1 Q Do you think Tom will pass his exams?

A – Of course he will.
　　　– He might do.
　　　　　– Mmm … maybe.
　　　　　　　– I doubt it.
　　　　　　　　　– No chance.

2 Q Does Martin earn a lot of money?

A – Yes, absolutely.
　　　– I think so.
　　　　　– Mmm … I'm not sure.
　　　　　　　– I don't think so.
　　　　　　　　　– Definitely not.

3 Q Are England going to win the World Cup?

A – Definitely!
　　　– Perhaps.
　　　　　– They might do.
　　　　　　　– Anything's possible.
　　　　　　　　　– Not a chance.

2 **T 5.14** Listen to the conversations. <u>Underline</u> the answers the two people give. Do they agree with each other?

3 **T 5.14** Listen again. Pay attention to the stress and intonation. Practise in groups of three. Choose your own replies.

4 Complete these conversations with a word or phrase from exercise 1.

1 A Kelly's job is really stressful, isn't it?

B _____ . She's a paramedic.

A Is she having a holiday soon?

B I _____ so. She says she _____ go to Spain.

2 A Isn't it Rob's birthday next week?

B Yes, _____ . It's on the 21st.

A So he's a Capricorn.

B No, I _____ . I think he's an Aquarius.

3 A Do you think Anita and Paul are in love?

B _____ . They're going to get married next June in Hawaii.

A Hawaii! Are you going to the wedding?

B _____ . I can't afford it.

T 5.15 Listen and compare.

5 Work in groups. Ask everyone in the group for their opinion.

1　Did Leo Tolstoy write *War and Peace*?
2　Is Nicole Kidman American?
3　Was Sherlock Holmes a real person?
4　Is the population of China more than 2 billion?
5　Do some vegetarians eat fish?
6　Is the weather going to be nice next weekend?
7　Are you going to be rich and famous one day?
8　Is your school the best in town?

T 5.16 Listen and compare.

6 The way I see it

What … like? • Comparatives and superlatives • Synonyms and antonyms • *What's on?*

STARTER

Look at the picture of Mia. Describe her.   *She's about 25. She's got … She's quite …*

TELL ME ABOUT HER
What's she like?

1 **T 6.1** Listen to four conversations about Mia. Which question …?

- asks about her health
- asks for a physical description
- uses *like* as a verb
- means *Tell me about her in general.*

1 'Do you like Mia?'
'Yes, I do. I like her a lot.'

3 'What's Mia like?'
'She's really nice. Very friendly.'

2 'How's Mia?'
'She's fine, thanks. Very well.'

4 'What does Mia look like?'
'She's tall, and she's got brown eyes and black hair.'

2 Think of more answers to the questions.

> Do you like Mia?

> Yes, she's my best friend.

> No, I can't stand her!

> She's all right.

Mia

3 Match a question in **A** with an answer in **B**.

A	B
1 What's your teacher like?	___ a Lovely! Warm and sunny.
2 What sports do you like?	___ b She's great! She helps us a lot.
3 What does your brother look like?	___ c They're OK. Busy as usual.
4 Do you like pizza?	___ d He's got blond hair and blue eyes.
5 What's the weather like today?	___ e Mmm, I love it!
6 How are your parents?	___ f Cycling and skiing.

T 6.2 Listen and check. Ask and answer the questions about you.

PRACTICE
What's it like?

1 Mia often travels in her job. She's talking to her friend, Tom, about Shanghai. Complete Tom's questions.

T What <u>'s Shanghai</u> _____ like?
M It's very big and noisy, but it's very exciting.
T What _____ like?
M It's the best in the world! I just love Chinese food!
T What _____ like?
M They're very friendly, and they really want to do business.
T What _____ like?
M When I was there, it was hot and humid.
T What _____ like?
M There are new buildings everywhere, but if you look hard, you can still find some older ones, too.

2 **T 6.3** Listen and check. Practise the conversation with a partner.

3 Ask and answer the same questions about the town or city you are in now.

Shanghai

Singapore

Dubai

SINGAPORE, SHANGHAI, AND DUBAI
Comparatives and superlatives

1 **T 6.4** Mia also went to Singapore and Dubai. Listen and complete some of the things she says.

THE CITY Singapore is older than Shanghai, but it's _____ smaller. Shanghai is _____ bigger than Singapore and _____ noisier too.

BUSINESS They're both top financial centres, but Singapore is _____ important. It's better for investment.

BUILDINGS AND PEOPLE Shanghai is more _____ than Singapore, but it isn't as cosmopolitan. Dubai is _____ newest and _____ city, and it's the most _____ .

CLIMATE Singapore is _____ than Shanghai. But it isn't _____ hot _____ Dubai. Dubai is the _____ place. Singapore is very humid, so it's _____ than Shanghai. But Dubai is the _____ . It only rains for a few days a year.

WHICH IS BEST? For me Shanghai is the _____ because it's the _____ and the _____ exciting.

2 **T 6.4** Listen again and check. What extra information do you hear?

3 What questions was Mia asked about each topic in exercise 1? Ask and answer them with a partner.

GRAMMAR SPOT

1 What are the comparative and superlative forms of these adjectives?

old	busy	big	important
small	noisy	wet	modern
new	dry	hot	exciting

When do we use *-er* and *-est*? When do we use *more* and *the most*?

2 These adjectives are irregular. What are the comparative and superlative forms?

   good   bad

3 Look at these patterns.

It **a bit/a little** bigger.   It's **a lot/much** smaller.
It's **isn't as** hot **as** Dubai.

▶▶ **Grammar Reference 6.1–6.2 p79**

PRACTICE

Pronunciation

1 **T 6.5** Listen and practise the sentences.

/ə/ / ə/
I'm older than Jane.

/ə/ /ə/
But I'm not as old as John.

/ɪ/
He's the oldest.

2 **T 6.6** Listen and practise the conversation with a partner.

Clever
A WHO's cleverer, YOU or BEN?
B ME, of course! I'm MUCH cleverer than Ben!
He isn't NEARLY as clever as ME!

Practise again using these adjectives.

| kind | funny | good-looking | ambitious |

T 6.7 Listen and compare.

Comparing people

3 Read the profiles of the four people. Complete the sentences comparing them.

1 Agnes has the <u>largest</u> family. She has _____ children. Kevin doesn't have _____ children _____ Agnes. He has just two.

2 Marilou is _____. She's 41. Marcel is _____. He's only 25. Agnes is a little bit _____ Kevin. She's 34, and he's 32.

3 Kevin works the _____ hours – 60 hours a week. Agnes doesn't work as _____ hours as Kevin, but she still works hard. She works _____ than Marcel, who only works 35 hours a week.

4 Kevin earns the _____. He has the _____ salary. Marilou has the _____ salary. Marcel doesn't earn anything like _____ Agnes. She earns nearly twice _____ as him.

5 Agnes has _____ house than Marilou, but it isn't _____ Kevin's. He has a huge house – six bedrooms! Marcel has _____ house.

4 Compare the two women. Then compare the two men.
Agnes is younger than Marilou.

5 Make sentences about their personalities. Compare two or three of them.
Marilou isn't as ..., but she's more ...

6 Work in small groups. Who do you think ...?

- has the most important job
- is the most creative
- is the busiest

Why do you think Agnes is the happiest?
Why is Marilou the unhappiest?

AGNES
from Sweden

LIFE DATA

Age: 34

Family:
Married, 3 children

Job:
Interior designer

Works hours/week:
50

Salary:
$75,000 a year

House:
4 bedrooms

PERSONALITY

Intelligent:
★★★★★

Ambitious:
★★★

Happy:
☺☺☺☺☺

KEVIN
from Chicago

LIFE DATA

Age: 32

Family:
Married, two sons

Job:
Financial advisor

Works hours/week:
60

Salary:
$100,000 a year

House:
6 bedrooms

PERSONALITY

Intelligent:
★★

Ambitious:
★★★★★

Happy:
☺☺☺

MARCEL
from France

LIFE DATA

Age: 25

Family:
Single

Job:
Cheese maker

Works hours/week:
35

Salary:
$40,000 a year

House:
2 bedrooms

PERSONALITY

Intelligent:
★★★

Ambitious:
★★

Happy:
☺☺☺☺

MARILOU
from the Philippines

LIFE DATA

Age: 41

Family:
Married, 1 daughter

Job:
Nurse

Works hours/week:
55

Salary:
$25,000 a year

House:
3 bedrooms

PERSONALITY

Intelligent:
★★★★

Ambitious:
★

Happy:
☺☺

LISTENING AND SPEAKING
My family

1 What are you like as a person?
Do any of these adjectives describe you?

messy	tidy	lazy	moody	noisy
kind	selfish	shy	ambitious	cheerful

2 **T 6.8** Listen to three people talking about their family.
Complete the chart.

Sally 20

Who is she like? _____

In what ways? _____

_____

_____

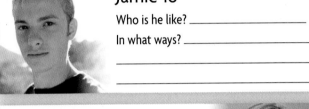

Jamie 16

Who is he like? _____

In what ways? _____

_____

Rachel 28

Who is she like? _____

In what ways? _____

_____

_____

3 How are these people different from each other?
- Sally and her sister, Lena
- Jamie and his twin brother, Rob
- Rachel and her father
- Rachel and her sister, Jenny

4 **T 6.8** Listen again. Complete the sentences.

Sally

1 We _____ films …
2 And she's _____ size as me.

Jamie

3 We're _____ character.
4 We _____ art.

Rachel

5 I hope I'm _____ him.

5 Who are *you* like in *your* family? Who do you look like?

READING AND SPEAKING
Multicultural London

1 What do you want from the country you live in? Put these qualities in order of importance for you (1 = most important).

- [ ] a safe and honest society
- [ ] a good education for children and adults
- [ ] the opportunity to find work and have a career
- [ ] a good place to bring up your children
- [ ] a society where people are free to say and do what they want

Talk with a partner, then in small groups. Discuss your answers as a class.

2 Read the introduction to the article. What is special about London? What is special about Stroud Green Road?

3 Look at the pictures and profiles of the people in the article. Where are they from? What are they doing in London?

4 Work in small groups. Choose two of the people. Read about them and answer the questions.

1 When and why did she/he come to England?
2 How did he/she find it at first?
3 What does she/he say about her/his business?
4 How does England compare to his/her own country?
5 What family does she/he talk about?
6 What does he/she think of living in England?
7 Does she/he intend to stay or go back home?

5 Find a student from another group. Compare and swap information.

6 Which of the qualities of a country in exercise 1 are important to the four people? Did they find these qualities in England?

What do you think?

- When people go to live in a foreign country, they can experience culture shock. What do you understand by this?
- Why do people leave their own country? What are they looking for? What are they escaping from?

Project

Find someone living in your country who is from a different country. What do they do? What do they think of living in your country? Bring the information to class and tell the other students.

▶▶ **WRITING** Describing my hometown *p62*

The world in

London is the most multicultural city in the world. On an ordinary street in north London, people from across the globe live and work side by side. Here on Stroud Green Road there are Turks, Chinese, Afghanis, Pakistanis, Vietnamese, Colombians, Polish, Kenyans, and French.

What are the thoughts of the people who live here? What do they think of the land they now call home?

PROFILE
Name Burkan Mehmet, 41
Born Istanbul, Turkey
Business The Sunflower Gallery

" This area is very cosmopolitan, and that's why I love it. When I first came to England in 1986, I thought it would be like New York, but it was much quieter. I didn't know anybody, and I wanted to go home.

I came here to study business at college. First I had a restaurant. Now I run this florist's shop. My customers come from so many different cultures – I learn something new every day.

What I like about England is that there's a system that works. Things are more organized here. I'm a British citizen now. When I go back to Turkey, I see how I've changed. Life in Turkey is faster, and more hectic than here.

I would like to go back to Istanbul one day. But for now, I love London. I'm married, and I have a daughter, Ceren. I wouldn't think of living anywhere else. "

one street

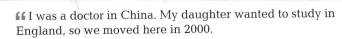

STROUD GREEN ROAD N4

PROFILE
Name Ming Liang Chen, 50
Born Qingdao, **China**
Business The Chinese Medical Centre

"I was a doctor in China. My daughter wanted to study in England, so we moved here in 2000.

Life for us here was impossible for the first few years. It was hard to find work. It was also difficult to talk to people. But things got easier as my English improved. People in the West are now more interested in herbal medicine.

My daughter is married and has a son and lives here. I see her every day. That is Chinese culture – children and parents stay together.

This is the big difference for us. In China we are surrounded by family. Here I feel like a foreigner. I miss my friends and colleagues, and my wife is very close to her family back home.

My daughter is settled here, but I think my wife and I will return to China. We'll see. "

PROFILE
Name Luz-Elena Lamprea, 41
Born Tuluá, **Colombia**
Business Los Guadales restaurant

"My parents divorced, and my mother came to England to make a new start. I was 19.

For me it was an enormous shock. When you are in Colombia, you think everything in Europe is wonderful. I arrived in September, the weather was awful and the skies were grey. London wasn't nearly as exciting as I thought.

I spent a year studying English, then fell in love. The marriage didn't work, but I had two children, Jennifer and Julian.

I bought this restaurant. It's becoming more and more popular, especially with Europeans. I love my work. It's the most interesting job in the world. I'm not just serving food, I'm giving people an experience of my culture.

I'm so thankful now that I came here. There is more opportunity. I go to Colombia every year, but when I'm there I miss England. I really love being here. "

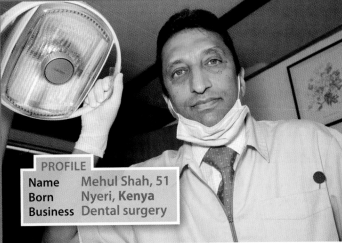

PROFILE
Name Mehul Shah, 51
Born Nyeri, **Kenya**
Business Dental surgery

"I always wanted to study medicine. I had an uncle in London, so when I was 16, I came here.

It was very hard. I remember the drive from the airport. The roads were so much bigger and busier than in Kenya. It was summer, and the weather was lovely. But then of course the first winter came. It was the coldest winter for years!

My patients are of all nationalities, all religions, all colours. I love it. I'm seeing the third generation of the same families.

This is a democratic country. You're free here, you can say and think, and do what you like.

England is a welcoming society. My children were born here. All their friends are English. I feel British now. I became a British citizen 24 years ago. Britain gave me an education and the opportunity to better myself. This is my country, my home. "

VOCABULARY
Synonyms and antonyms

1 Look at the extract from the text on page 51.

> "It was hard to find work. It was also difficult to talk to people. But things got easier ... "

Which words are synonyms?
Which words are antonyms (opposites)?

2 We use synonyms and antonyms because we don't want to repeat words. What's wrong with this conversation?

A It's a lovely day, isn't it?
B Yes, it's *lovely*!
A But it wasn't very *lovely* yesterday, was it?
B No, it wasn't *lovely*.

Try the conversation again using the words *beautiful*, *nice*, and *horrible*.

Synonyms

3 Complete the conversations with a synonym in the box.

tiny	clever	annoyed	wealthy	fed up	pleased

1 'Jane comes from a very rich family.'
  'Really? I knew her uncle was very _____.'

2 'Was Sophie angry when you were late?'
  'Yeah. She was pretty _____, it's true.'

3 'Jack's such an intelligent boy!'
  'Mm. He's very _____ for a ten-year old.'

4 'I've had enough of winter now.'
  'I know. I'm _____ with all these dark nights.'

5 'Dave and Sarah's flat is small, isn't it?'
  'Mm. It's _____. I don't know how they live there.'

6 'Are you happy with your new car?'
  'Yes, I'm very _____ with it. It goes really well.'

T 6.9 Listen and check. What's the extra line of each conversation?

4 Think of another word for these adjectives.

good-looking	amazing	crazy	big
new	old	awful	cold

5 Work in pairs. Write sentences using an adjective in exercise 4. Read them to another group. They must reply using a synonym.

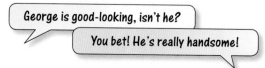

George is good-looking, isn't he?

You bet! He's really handsome!

Antonyms

6 We can agree with people by using *not very* + an antonym.

A Tom's so messy!
B Yes, teenagers aren't very tidy, are they?

7 Think of a word that means the opposite of these adjectives.

easy	<u>difficult</u>	naughty	_____
noisy	_____	exciting	_____
miserable	_____	clever	_____
polite	_____	clean	_____

8 Agree with these sentences using antonyms.

1 That man was so rude to me!

  Yes, he wasn't very polite, was he?

2 Some people are so stupid!
3 Dave's flat is always so dirty!
4 His wife always looks so miserable!
5 Their children are so naughty!
6 This lesson is boring!

T 6.10 Listen and compare. Practise the conversations.

EVERYDAY ENGLISH

What's on?

1 Read the listings and find the answers to these questions.
- How much is it to go in the British Museum?
- Is the Van Gogh exhibition open on Sunday?
- How many nights is the concert on at the Royal Festival Hall?
- What film is suitable for young children?
- Is *The Phantom of the Opera* popular? How do you know?

2 **T 6.11** Listen and complete the conversations.

1 A What shall we do today?
  B I'm not sure. How about _____ ?
  A Mmm ... I don't really feel like _____ .

2 B OK. Would you like to go to an exhibition?
  A That sounds interesting! _____ ?
  B Well, there's a Van Gogh exhibition.
  A Is it _____ ?
  B I think it _____ really good!

3 A _____ ?
  B It's on at the Royal Academy.
  A What's the _____ ?
  B Piccadilly Circus.
  A How much is it?
  B It's _____ students.
  A What time is it open?
  B From ten till six.
  A Right! _____ !

3 **T 6.11** Listen again. Practise the conversations in pairs.

4 Work with a partner. Have similar conversations about other things to do.

5 Imagine you are in London for a weekend. You and your partner have £50 each to spend on going out. Talk together and decide what you want to do.

Listings

Time Out London

British Museum
44 Great Russell Street, WC1B 3DG
⊖ Russell Sq
10am–5.30pm
FREE
Exhibitions
Chinese Vases Pottery from the Ming Dynasty 1368–1644
South American Indians The gold and silver of the Incas
Ancient Egypt Statues of kings, pharaohs, and gods

Peruvian Inca gold

Royal Academy Of Arts
Burlington House, Piccadilly, W1J OBD
020 7300 8000
⊖ Piccadilly Circus
Exhibition
The Real Van Gogh: the Artist and his Letters
10am – 6pm daily
£12; £10 seniors;
£8 students; under 7s free.
Booking 0844 209 1919
Van Gogh's artistic development is revealed in his private letters.

Royal Festival Hall
Southbank Centre, Belvedere Road, SE11 8XX
0844 875 0073
⊖ Waterloo
Concert
Beethoven's Pastoral Symphony
Thurs 4th only; 7.30pm
£6 – £20
The Paddington Symphony orchestra perform one of the world's most popular symphonies.

Odeon Cinema Piccadilly Circus
19 Regent St, SW1Y 4LR
0871220 6000
⊖ Piccadilly Circus
before 5pm £10;
after 5pm £13
Films
The Survivors (15)
10.40am, 1.50, 4.00, 6.10, 8.20, 10.30
Family fights to live after nuclear war destroys world.
My Favourite Fairy (U)
10.00am, 12.15pm, 3.00, 5.30
Dolls and toys come alive in a girl's bedroom.
Final Solution (18)
12.40pm, 3.50, 6.15, 8.30, 11.10
Drugs, murder, violence in New York crime gang.

Her Majesty's Theatre
Haymarket and Charles II St, SW1Y 4QL
0844 579 1940
⊖ Piccadilly Circus
Musical
The Phantom of the Opera
Mon – Sat 7.30pm; Tues and Sat matinee 2.30pm.
£20 – £55. Runs 2hrs 30 mins. Booking recommended. Andrew Lloyd Webber's musical in its 24th year. A heartbreaking story of love.

TIME OUT London

Writing contents

Reference materials

Writing

1 Look at the symbols often used to correct mistakes in writing. Correct the <u>underlined</u> mistakes in the sentences. Compare your answers with a partner.

Sp	Spelling	1 I'm <u>enjoing</u> the party. ^{Sp}
WW	Wrong word	2 They went <u>in</u> Italy on holiday. ^{WW}
WO	Word order	3 I have <u>two brothers younger</u>. ^{WO}
Gr	Grammar	4 She's got some new <u>reds</u> shoes. ^{Gr}
T	Tense	5 He <u>arrive</u> yesterday. ^T
P	Punctuation	6 They <u>arent</u> coming. ^P
⋀	Word missing	7 She's ⋀ doctor.

2 Work in two groups. In each of the sentences below there is one mistake.

Group A Find the mistakes in **A**. Use the symbols to mark them, but don't correct them.

Group B Find the mistakes in **B**. Use the symbols to mark them, but don't correct them.

A
1 I like Rome because is a beautiful city.
2 She studied for three years psychology.
3 There aren't any milk.
4 He's speaking French, German, and Spanish.
5 I watched TV, than I went to bed.
6 Did you by any bread at the supermarket?

B
1 I lost my all money.
2 What did you last night?
3 He always wear jeans.
4 My town is quite at the weekend.
5 I want that I pass the exam.
6 She's married with Peter.

3 Find a partner from the other group. Correct each other's sentences.

4 Correct this piece of student writing.

My best friend

My best friend was my best man when I <u>get</u> married two ^T
^{Gr} ^{Gr} ^{WW}
<u>year</u> ago. <u>He's</u> name is Antonio and we met <u>in</u> university in

Bologna. In fact we met on our very first day <u>their</u>. Antonio ^{Sp}
^{WW}
was ⋀ first person I spoke <u>with</u> and we discovered we were

both studying Spanish and that we were both football
^{WO}
fans. When we left university we went <u>together travelling</u>
^{Gr} ^P
for six <u>month</u>. We had a fantastic time touring <u>north</u> and
^P ^P
<u>south america</u>. When we were in Mexico we met two sisters
^{WW} ^{WW}
<u>of</u> London, Emma and Kate. Now I'm married <u>with</u> Emma

and next year Antonio and Kate ⋀ going to get married. I like
^{Gr}
Antonio because he ⋀ very funny and we <u>has</u> really good
^{Gr}
times together. He <u>live</u> in a different town now, but we text
^{WO}
or call <u>often each other</u>. I'm very lucky that he's my friend.

5 Write about your own best friend.

6 Swap with a partner and see if you can find any mistakes. Read your work aloud to the class.

1 Read the postcard. Where are Gemma and Martin? Are they enjoying their holiday? Why? What is wrong with the style of the writing?

Dear Melanie,

Here we are in New York having a nice time. The weather is very nice. We're staying in quite a nice hotel in a nice part of town, Lower Manhattan. We've got a nice view of the Empire State Building from our bedroom window. We think all the skyscrapers are nice. Yesterday we went on a really nice helicopter tour of the city and then in the evening we saw a nice show on Broadway. Today we are going shopping in Bloomingdale's. It's a nice store for buying clothes. This evening we're going to eat at Michael Jordan's 'The Steak House' in Grand Central Station. The restaurants here are nice and the food is really nice, but the portions are so huge that we often can't finish the meal.

See you soon,

Love,

Gemma and Martin

Melanie Baker
10 Wallasey Road
Brentwood,
Essex
CM15 7LE
ENGLAND

2 Gemma and Martin use *nice* eleven times. Complete the sentences below with other adjectives from the box. Sometimes more than one adjective is possible, but not always!

great	warm and sunny	interesting	excellent
delicious	luxurious	spectacular	amazing
exciting	brilliant	wonderful	

1 We're having a/an _____ time here in New York.

2 The weather is _____ .

3 We're staying in a/an _____ hotel in a/an _____ part of town.

4 We have _____ views of the Empire State Building.

5 We think the skyscrapers are _____ .

6 We went on a/an _____ helicopter ride.

7 In the evening we saw a/an _____ show.

8 Bloomingdale's is a/an _____ store for buying clothes.

9 The restaurants here are _____ .

10 The food here is really _____ .

3 Work with a partner. Read the postcard aloud using a variety of adjectives. Use *nice* once only. Discuss where you think is the best place to use it.

4 Think of a holiday you once had. Imagine you are still there. Write a postcard to an English friend about it, but use the adjective *nice* once only! You can write about some of these things:

- the journey
- the weather
- the accommodation
- the food
- some things you did yesterday
- some things you are going to do today

Compare postcards with your partner then read them to the class.

1 Work with a partner. Look at the picture story. What is it about?

The burglar who fell asleep z ᶻ Z ᶻ Z Z Z Z

2 Read the sentences. They tell the story. Put the words in *italics* in a suitable position in the sentence. Change the punctuation if necessary.

1 A burglar broke into a house in Paris.
   Last Sunday evening *large, expensive* *in the centre of*
   Last Sunday evening, a burglar broke into a large, expensive house in the centre of Paris.

2 He went into the living room and he filled his sack with all the silverware and a Chinese vase.
   First *quickly and quietly* *priceless*

3 He went to the kitchen and found some cheese and two bottles of champagne.
   Next *delicious* *the best*

4 He was feeling hungry and thirsty. He ate the cheese and drank the champagne.
   extremely *so* *all*

5 He felt very tired. He went to the bedroom and lay down on a big bed, and fell asleep.
   Suddenly *upstairs* *comfortable* *immediately* *fast*

6 He slept very well. When he woke up, three policemen were standing round his bed.
   Unfortunately *the next morning*

T 3.13 Listen and check.

3 The pictures below illustrate a news story. What is it about? Match notes 1–6 with the pictures.

1 The phone was smelly and dirty. It still worked. Glen called some numbers.

2 Andrew Cheatle, a businessman from Worthing in Sussex, was walking on the beach. He lost his mobile. **(a)**

3 He was preparing the fish for sale. He noticed something metal inside a cod fish. It was a mobile phone.

4 One week later, fisherman, Glen Kerley, was on his boat catching fish to sell in the market.

5 Glen returned the phone to Andrew. He still uses it.

6 Andrew was with his girlfriend, Rita Smith. Her mobile phone rang. She said, 'It's for you! It's a call from your phone.'

A fishy tale

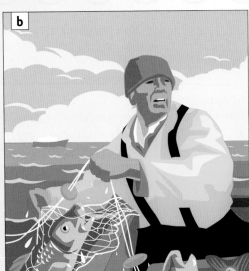

4 Write the news story. Use suitable words to join the ideas and to make the story more interesting. Compare your stories in groups and with the sample answer on p86.

1 You receive an email from an old friend. It is many years since you heard from them. You want to reply and tell them about you and your life. Make some notes.

but, *although*, and *however*

2 Read these sentences. They all mean the same, but how are they different?

- I don't write many letters, **but** I send a lot of emails.
- **Although** I don't write many letters, I send a lot of emails.
- I don't write many letters. **However**, I send a lot of emails.

3 Join these pairs of sentences in different ways.

1 I love ice cream. I don't eat it often.
2 He's a good friend. We don't have a lot in common.
3 She isn't English. She speaks English very well.
4 It rained a lot. We enjoyed the holiday.

so and *because*

4 Read these sentences.

1 He lived in France for many years, **so** he speaks French well.
2 He speaks French well **because** he lived in France for many years.

Which pattern goes with which sentence?

a Result ──────────▶ Cause
b Cause ──────────▶ Result

5 Join the pairs of sentences in two different ways using *so* and *because*.

1 I don't eat broccoli. I don't like it.
2 She went home. She was tired.
3 We didn't enjoy our holiday. The weather was bad.
4 He worked hard. He passed all his exams.
5 I enjoy history lessons. I like the teacher.
6 It started to rain. We stopped playing tennis.

6 Read the email. Who is writing to who? Why? What news does she give? Complete the email with these linking words.

| but   although   however   so   because |

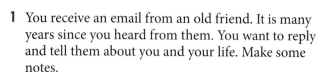

```
○○○
Date:      Wed, 27 Apr. 20:07:36 +0100 (BST)
From:      "Lindy Cameron" <lindy.cam5@donwana.com>
Subject:   RE: Do you remember me?
To:        "Teresa Tate" <Teresa@Tate174.fsnet.co.uk>
```

Dear Teresa,

How wonderful to hear from you. Of course I remember you (1) _____ it's nearly seven years since we were neighbours. How did you get my email address? You told me a little about you and your family, (2) _____ now I'd like to know more. You ask how we all are, (3) _____ here's some of our news.

First things first – George and I are now divorced! I know you never liked him much, (4) _____ you are probably not too surprised. (5) _____, we still see each other a lot (6) _____ of the twins. They're nine now and they're good girls, (7) _____, of course, sometimes a bit of a handful. We moved from Birmingham (8) _____ I didn't want them to grow up in a big city. We now live in a beautiful, old farmhouse in Wales. I love country life. We have lots of land, (9) _____ we grow all our own vegetables and keep a few chickens. (10) _____, it's all very expensive to look after and (11) _____ I sell some of our produce to the local shops, we never have enough money for holidays and treats, (12) _____ we're happy and healthy.

I can't wait to hear more of your news. Write very soon.

Please come to stay. I'd love to see you again.

Love
Lindy X

7 Write an email to your old friend. Use your notes from exercise 1 and the phrases below. Compare your email with your partner's.

Dear X
How wonderful/amazing to hear from you.
I was so surprised./What a wonderful surprise.
How did you get my email address?
It was great to get your news.
Let me tell you something about my life.
Please let's keep in touch.
Love/Best wishes/All the best

1 Think about your future. How do you see your life …?

- next year
- in five years' time
- in ten years' time
- when you're 40 or 50

Write some notes about your hopes and ambitions at each of these times. Tell the class.

2 **T 5.5** Read and listen to Susannah talking about her future. What are her definite plans? What is she not sure about? What are her hopes, ambitions, and dreams?

3 Read Susannah's talk again carefully. Underline any words or expressions that would be useful when you write a talk about your future. Compare with your partner. Have you chosen the same ones?

4 Rewrite the first paragraph about you. Read it aloud.

5 Write a talk about your future plans and dreams. Mark pauses and words you want to stress. Practise reading it aloud. Give your talk to the class. Answer any questions.

My dreams for the future

Hello everyone. My name's Susannah – Susie for short. I'm 20 years old. At the moment I'm in my second year at art school and I often dream about my future. I have big plans and I'd like to tell you a bit about them.

My most immediate plans are holiday plans. I'm going to visit my brother who's working in Australia. My mother and I are going to spend Christmas with him in the summer sun. I'm very excited about that.

When I return I need to make a final decision about which course to study next year. I'm still not sure – I'm thinking of doing either fashion design or landscape design. It's difficult because I'm interested in both clothes and gardens. If I choose landscape I'd like to work with my friend, Jasper. He's brilliant with gardens and we've already worked on two together. It was great fun and we get on very well.

In five or ten years' time I would like to have my own business and work for myself like my father. He has his own building business. Perhaps I'll do a business course after I finish art school.

Of course, one day I hope to marry and have children. Ideally before I'm 30, but I can't plan when I'll meet the right person and I haven't got a boyfriend at the moment.

In my dreams I see myself at 40 running a successful gardening company with about 20 employees. I'll design beautiful gardens for beautiful people. I'll have a beautiful house, two beautiful children, and of course a husband who's as successful as I am. Who knows, it could even be Jasper!

1 Complete this sentence in any way you can.

The town where I was born is / has …

Share the information with the class.

GRAMMAR SPOT

1 We use *who*, *that*, *which*, and *where* to join sentences. Look at these sentences.

I met a man. He is from my town.
I met a man **who** is from my town.

I bought a house. It's in Market Street.
I bought a house **which/that** is in Market Street.

The hotel was very comfortable. We stayed in it.
The hotel **where** we stayed was very comfortable.

2 *Who*, *which*, *that*, and *where* are relative pronouns. Complete the rules with a relative pronoun.

- _____ is for people.
- _____ or _____ is for things.
- _____ is for places.

---

2 Join the sentences with the correct relative pronoun.

1 There's the boy. He broke the window.
2 That's the palace. The Queen lives there.
3 There are the policemen. They caught the thief.
4 I bought a watch. It stopped after two days.
5 Here are the letters. They arrived this morning.
6 That's the hospital. I was born in it.

3 Look at the pictures of Pittsburgh. What do you learn about the town from them? Read the text and complete it with *who*, *which/that*, or *where*. Answer the questions.

1 Where is the town?
2 How many bridges are there?
3 Who is the city named after?
4 What was it like 50 years ago?
5 What is it like now?
6 Which artists come from Pittsburgh?
7 What are the people like?

4 Write a similar description of your hometown in about 200 words. First write some notes about it.

- Where is it?   • What's its history?   • What's it like now?

Next write some personal opinions.

- Do you like it?   • Why?/Why not?

5 Read some descriptions aloud and compare your towns.

PITTSBURGH
THE TOWN WHERE I WAS BORN

I was born in Pittsburgh, the second largest city in Pennsylvania, USA, with a population of about 2.4 million. Pittsburgh lies on the banks of three rivers (1) ___*that*___ are crossed by over 400 bridges. The city is named after William Pitt, (2) _____ was the Prime Minister of Britain in the 1700s. It is sometimes called 'The City of Bridges'.

Fifty years ago, Pittsburgh was a thriving, industrial town. It had dozens of factories (3) _____ produced iron and steel. However, in the 1970s and 80s the steel mills closed and the city suffered badly. Streets, (4) _____ once people hurried to work, became deserted and dangerous. However, today, a lot of these streets are thriving again with theatres, shops, and restaurants.

Pittsburgh is surrounded by hills from (5) _____ you can enjoy great views of the city, views (6) _____ have inspired many artists, such as Linda Barnicott, who painted *My Home Town*. The museums display the work of many local artists, including Andy Warhol, (7) _____ was born and raised in Pittsburgh.

The city is now named one of the 'World's Most Liveable Cities'. I moved away ten years ago, but I often return. I miss the tough, friendly people, (8) _____ have lived through good times and bad. They make me proud to call Pittsburgh my hometown.

Linda Barnicott's *My Home Town*

Tapescripts

UNIT 1

T 1.1

A Where were you born?
B In Scotland.
A What do you do?
B I'm a teacher.
A Are you married?
B No, I'm not.
A Why are you learning English?
B Because I need it for my job.
A When did you start learning English?
B Two years ago.
A How often do you have English classes?
B Twice a week.

T 1.2 Anton Kristoff from Toronto, Canada

Hi! I'm Anton. I come from Canada, but at the moment I'm living here in New York. I'm working as a bike messenger. I really like New York, it's the center of the universe and it's very cosmopolitan. I have friends from all over the world. I earn about $100 a day in this job. That's good money. I'm saving money for my education.
I was born in Toronto, but my parents are from Bulgaria. They moved to Canada thirty years ago. When they first arrived they didn't speak any English. They worry about me. Last month I had a bad accident on my bike, but I'm fine now. Next September I'm going back home to Toronto, and I'm going to study for a Master's degree and then I hope to get a good job.

T 1.3 Rowenna Lee from Melbourne, Australia

Hi, I'm Rowenna. I'm Australian, I come from Melbourne, but now I live in north London with my husband David. He's English. David and I run an art gallery. It's a gallery for Australian Aboriginal art. I just love Aboriginal art, I love all the colours and shapes. I'm preparing a new exhibition at the moment.
I came to England in 2006 as a student. My parents wanted me to study law, but I didn't like it, -er, I hated it in fact. I left the course after three months and got a job in an art gallery, that's where I met David. Then, we had the idea of opening our own gallery just for Aboriginal art, because most English people don't know anything about it. That was in 2006, and we borrowed £25,000 from the bank to do it. We're lucky because the gallery's really successful and we paid the money back after just five years. I go back to Australia every year. I usually go in the English winter because it's summer in Australia. But I'm not going next year because, you see, I'm going to have a baby in December. It's my first so I'm very excited.

T 1.4 Questions about Rowenna

1 A Where does she live?
   B In north London.
   A Who with?
   B With her husband, David.
2 A What does she do?
   B She runs an art gallery.
3 A What's she doing at the moment?
   B She's preparing a new art exhibition
4 A When and why did she come to England?
   B She came to England in 2006 to study law.
5 A How long did she study law?
   B For three months.
6 A How much money did she borrow from the bank?
   B £25,000.
7 A How many children does she have?
   B She doesn't have any at the moment.
8 A Why is she excited?
   B Because she's going to have a baby.

T 1.5 Questions to Serkan

I Hi, Serkan. Nice to meet you. Can I ask you one or two questions?
S Yes, of course.
I First of all, where do you come from?
S I'm from Istanbul in Turkey.
I And why are you here in England?
S Well, I'm here mainly because I want to improve my English.
I How much English did you know before you came?
S Not a lot. I studied English at school, but I didn't learn much. Now I'm studying in a language school here.
I Which school?
S The Shakespeare School of English.
I A good name! Your English is very good now. Who's your teacher?
S Thank you very much. My teacher's called David. He's great.
I What did you do back in Turkey?
S Well, actually, I was a teacher, a history teacher. I taught children from 14 to 18.
I How many children were in your classes?
S Sometimes as many as 40.
I Goodness! That's a lot. How often do you go back home?
S Usually I go every two months, but this month my brother is coming here. I'm very excited. I'm going to show him round.
I Well, I hope your brother has a great visit.

T 1.6 *Who's* or *Whose*?

1 A Whose phone is ringing?
   B It's mine.
2 A Who's calling?
   B It's my brother.

T 1.7

1 A Whose phone is ringing?
   B It's mine.
2 A Who's calling?
   B It's my brother.
3 Who's on the phone?
4 I'm going to the pub. Who's coming?
5 Whose coat is this? It's not mine.
6 Whose are all these CDs?
7 Who's going to Tina's wedding?
8 Do you know whose glasses they are?

T 1.8 Questions about you

1 What do you like doing in your free time?
2 Do you like listening to music?
3 What kind of music do you like?
4 What did you do last weekend?
5 What are you doing tonight?
6 What are you going to do after this lesson?
7 How many languages does your teacher speak?
8 What's your teacher wearing today?

T 1.9 Listen and compare

A What do you like doing in your free time?
B I like being with my friends. We go to each other's houses and chat.
A Do you like listening to music?
B Yes, of course. I have an iPod.
A What kind of music do you like?
B I like all kinds, rock, jazz, pop, but the thing I like best is listening to my dad's old *Beatles* albums.
A What did you do last weekend?
B It was my mum's birthday so we all cooked a special meal for her.
A What are you doing tonight?
B Nothing much. I want to get an early night before the weekend.
A What are you going to do after this lesson?
B I have a bit of shopping to do. Then I'm going home.
A How many languages does your teacher speak?
B Only English! She says she's going to learn Italian next year.
A What's your teacher wearing today?
B A very pink jumper and red trousers. Mmm – not a great look!

T 1.10 **My oldest friend**

1 Kenny talking to Judy

J Kenny, I see you have more than 300 friends on Facebook!

K Amazing, isn't it? I don't know how it happened. I think it's because my job takes me all over the world and I make friends wherever I go.

J I travel too, but I don't have that many friends.

K Come on Judy. I'm your friend, that's one friend at least!

J But what about close friends? How many of the 300 are close?

K I have no idea.

J No idea? More than ten? More than twenty?

K Er, probably no more than ten really close friends.

J So, who's your oldest friend?

K That's easy. Pete's my oldest friend – since we were both 16, and he came to my school. He lives in Canada now. But he was best man at my wedding and I was best man at his.

J How often do you see him?

K Not often. Maybe once or twice a year. I went over to Canada last year when his son was born. Do you know, he named him Ken after me?

J Hey, that's lovely! You and Pete are really good friends, aren't you?

K Yeah!

J Why do you think that is?

K It's our love of football!

J Don't tell me, he supports Liverpool too!

K Of course. Best team in the world. No, seriously the best thing about Pete is that maybe we don't see each other for months, even years, but when we get together immediately we're talking …

J … about football.

K No, about all kinds of things. Our families mainly. He's a great guy.

2 Damian talking to Toby

T Am I your best friend?

D No, silly, you're my brother!

T I'm not silly. Can't I be your best friend?

D No, you can't. No one's best friends with his brother!

T But I don't have many friends.

D That's *your* problem. Look, I'm going to meet Thomas and the gang now.

T Is Thomas your best friend?

D No.

T Is he your oldest friend?

D No. Zac's my oldest friend. You know that – since we sat next to each other in Class 1. Zac and me are going to travel the world together when we finish school.

T Can I come?

D NO, YOU CAN'T! Just shut …

T Well, can Thomas be my friend?

D Toby, be quiet about friends! You are so boring, I'm not surprised you have no friends.

T But can I …?

D No, no, no! I'm off. See you!

T But …

3 Katie talking to Beth

B Katie, you're lucky, you have so many friends!

K Mmm, I suppose so. I do have quite a lot.

B Why do think that is?

K Well, I'm not sure, I think I kind of collect friends. I have friends from all different times in my life. You know school, university, and now at work, and I keep my friends.

B So, who's your oldest friend?

K You are, of course! You and me, Beth, we're the same age, 24, and you could say we met before we were born.

B I suppose you're right …

K Yeah, our mums met when they were …

B I know they met at the hospital when they went for check-ups before we were born.

K Yeah, and we were born on the same day.

B I know, but I'm ten hours older than you!

K That's why you're wiser than me! You're my oldest and my best friend. You're like a sister to me.

T 1.11 **A survey – How do couples meet?**

A survey of over 10,000 couples asked them how they first met. The top three were: first, with 22%, 'at work'; second, with 20%, 'through friends', and third, with 15%, 'at school or university'. Next, with 12%, was 'meeting online'. Nowadays more and more couples are meeting this way. Just 8% met at a bar or club and 5% through the family, which was quite surprising. Only 4% met on a blind date – perhaps not so surprising. Last of all, just 1% met while shopping – so don't go looking for love in the supermarket. That leaves just 13% who didn't meet in any of these places.

T 1.12 **What happened next?**

Dominic

I sent Sally a text a couple of days after the date. She played it cool and didn't reply for two days. We met up a week later, went for a walk, and then to the cinema. We're still seeing each other. She's helping me train for the marathon which is next month. She's going to come and watch me. Also, she came to the theatre to watch my play and she said she liked it. I'm going to meet her parents next weekend. I'm a bit worried about that, but I enjoy being with her a lot.

Sally

When Dom texted, I knew I wanted to answer, but I made him wait. I'm not sure why, silly really because I really do like him. I enjoyed seeing him act. I think he's a very good actor, but I didn't really understand the play. He's coming to meet my family next weekend. I don't usually take my boyfriends home so soon, but with Dom it's different. I have a good feeling about this relationship. Will it last? Ask me again a year from now!

T 1.13 **Words with two meanings**

1 Turn **left** in the High Street and my house is first on the right.
   She **left** hurriedly to catch her bus.

2 I love travelling by **train**.
   He's going to **train** for the marathon.

3 I'm going to **run** a marathon next month.
   They **run** the art gallery together.

4 I'm working at home for the **rest** of the week.
   I need a **rest**! I'm so tired.

5 What **kind** of books do you like reading?
   How **kind** of you to bring me some flowers!

6 Our **flat**'s on the fourth floor of a big apartment block.
   Holland is a very **flat** country.

7 What do you **mean**? I don't understand you.
   He never even buys me a coffee. He's very **mean**.

T 1.14 **Listen and repeat**

1 A Hi, Anna. How are you?
   B I'm fine, thanks. How are you?

2 A Thank you so much.
   B My pleasure.

3 A Can I help you?
   B No, thank you. I'm just looking.

4 A Excuse me! Is that seat free?
   B No, sorry. I'm afraid it isn't.

T 1.15 **Social expressions**

1 A Good morning!
   B Good morning! Lovely day again!

2 A See you tomorrow!
   B Yeah! About 9.00, in the coffee bar.

3 A How do you do?
   B How do you do? Pleased to meet you.

4 A Thank you very much indeed.
   B My pleasure. Don't mention it.

5 A I'm sorry. I can't come tonight.
   B Never mind. Perhaps another time.

6 A Can you help me with this exercise?
   B Of course. What's the problem?

7 A Bye!
   B Bye! See you later!

8 A Bye! Have a good weekend!
   B Thanks! Same to you.

9 A Sorry I'm late.
   B It doesn't matter. You're here now.

10 A Cheers!
   B Cheers! Here's to your new job!

T 1.16 **Conversations**

1 A Good morning!
   B Good morning! Lovely day again.
   A Yes, it's really warm for the time of year.

2 A See you tomorrow!
   B Yeah! About 9.00, in the coffee bar.
   A Fine. 9.00 is good for me, too.

3 A How do you do?
   B How do you do? Pleased to meet you.
   A Pleased to meet you, too.

4 A Thank you very much indeed.
   B My pleasure. Don't mention it.
   A It was so kind of you.

5 A I'm sorry. I can't come tonight.
   B Never mind. Perhaps another time.
   A I'm free tomorrow night. What about that?

6 A Can you help me with this exercise?
   B Of course. What's the problem?
   A I don't know what this word means.

7 A Bye!
   B Bye! See you later!
   A Yes. Let's meet after class.

8 A Bye! Have a good weekend!
   B Thanks! Same to you.
   A Thanks. Are you doing anything special?

9 A Sorry I'm late.
   B It doesn't matter. You're here now.
   A Yeah, I missed the bus.

10 A Cheers!
   B Cheers! Here's to your new job!
   A Thanks a lot. I'm excited, but a bit nervous.

UNIT 2

T 2.1 **Mamy Rock, The Granny DJ**

Ruth Flowers is not an ordinary grandmother. She's in her 70s, and has silver hair and bright-red lipstick. She's a DJ and works in clubs in Europe and tours festivals.

She lives alone in Bristol. She says, 'I've got a son and a grandson. They think what I'm doing is very cool!'

She likes rock bands such as Queen and the Rolling Stones, but she also plays electro and dance music. 'I love being with young people,' she says. 'They've got so much energy and enthusiasm!'

She's planning another European tour, and is currently making a new single. 'I'm having a lot of fun,' she says. 'I don't want it to stop.'

T 2.2 **The SuperJam millionaire**

Fraser Doherty is an extraordinary young man. He has his own company, SuperJam, which he started when he was just 16. 'I earn more money than my parents,' he says. His company makes jam – 500,000 jars every year – using a secret recipe from his grandmother.

All the major supermarkets sell his products. The business is growing fast – four flavours at the moment, but more on the way. And he has a charity that organizes huge tea parties for old people with live music and dancing.

'At the moment I'm very busy. I'm writing a cookbook. I've got an idea for a TV programme. And we're trying to get into the American market.'

T 2.3

Ruth Flowers

A What does Ruth do?
B She's a DJ.
A Where does she work?
B She works in clubs in Europe.
A How many children does she have?
B She has one son, and she also has a grandson.
A What sort of music does she like?
B She likes Queen and the Rolling Stones, and she also likes electro and dance music.
A Why does she like young people so much?
B Because they're so energetic and enthusiastic.
A What's she doing at the moment?
B She's planning another European tour, and she's making a new single.

Fraser Doherty

A What does Fraser do?
B He has his own company that makes jam.
A How much does he earn?
B He earns more than his parents.
A How many jars of jam does he make every year?
B He makes half a million jars a year.
A Whose recipe does he use?
B His grandmother's. It's a secret recipe.
A What's he writing?
B He's writing a cookbook.
A What's he trying to do?
B He's trying to get into the American market.

T 2.4 **An interview with Ruth**

I = Interviewer, R = Ruth

I Do you like being famous?
R Don't be silly. I'm not really famous. I'm just an old lady who's having fun.
I But it is unusual for someone your age, if you don't mind me saying, to be DJing in clubs for young people.
R Well, I just like the music. And I don't want to be an old woman in an old people's home watching television all day long and going to church once a week.
I Why do you do it?
R I DJ because the energy is fantastic! Because I love to see young people enjoying themselves. Because it makes me happy!
I Does your family agree with you?
R My family thinks it's great. Some of my friends say that it's not right for a woman my age to be wearing these clothes and staying out all night.
I And what do you say to them?
R I say it's none of their business. It doesn't matter how old you are. If you want to do something, you can.

T 2.5 **An interview with Fraser**

I = Interviewer, F = Fraser

I Do you like being a businessman?
F Oh, yes, I love it! I like the planning, the marketing, the selling. I like meeting people and talking about my business and everything about it!
I It seems to me you really love what you're doing!
F It's true! I do!
I Do you have any free time?
F Er … a bit, but not a lot.
I What do you do in your free time?
F I go out with my friends. I go to clubs. I love walking.
I Have you got a girlfriend?
F Well, er … that's none of your business!
I Sorry. Er … Who do you live with?
F I live with a group of friends in a flat in Edinburgh. It's not far from my parents' house.
I Do you see much of your parents?
F I see them all the time. We're very close.

T 2.6

A Do you have a car?
B Yes, I do.
C No, I don't.
A Have you got a bike?
B Yes, I have.
C No, I haven't.
D I don't have a camera.
E I haven't got an iPod.

T 2.7 **Things I like doing**

play games on my PlayStation
go out with my friends
download music and films
send emails and texts
shop for clothes online
have a lie-in
relax in front of the TV
meet friends for a drink
listen to music
go out for a meal
get a takeaway pizza
do nothing
read magazines
chat to friends online
go to the gym
watch a football match live on TV

T 2.8 **Listen, check, and practise**

1 I like shopping in the High Street, but mainly I shop online.
2 When I hear a band I like, I download their music from the Internet.
3 I listen to music on my iPod when I go jogging.
4 I spend hours chatting to friends online, even though I'm with them all day at school!
5 Sometimes I like to chill out at home and do nothing.
6 I'm always so tired after work I just want to relax in front of the TV.
7 On Saturdays, I have a lie-in, and don't get up till midday.
8 Do you want to cook tonight, or shall we get a takeaway pizza?
9 It's Pete's birthday tonight, so we're going out for a meal. Indian, I think.
10 I like keeping fit. I go to the gym three times a week.

T 2.9 **Money**

The best things in life are free
But you can give them to the birds and bees
I want money
That's what I want
That's what I want
Your love gives me such a thrill
But your love won't pay my bills
I want money

T 2.10 **Two neighbours**

Mrs Crumble

I have the flat above that young man. I think his name is Alfie Smith, because I see the postman delivering his letters. He never says hello.

He hasn't got a job, well he doesn't go out to work at 8.00 in the morning, and that's for sure! He doesn't get up till the afternoon, and he wears jeans and a T-shirt all the time. He never looks smart. He certainly never wears a suit. Goodness knows where he gets his money from! It's funny! I never hear him in the evening. I've no idea what he does in the evening.

There are people coming and going in and out of his flat all day long. I have no idea how many people are staying. Four? Five? Have none of them got jobs?

He's got a girlfriend. She's very … pretty. Blond hair, dyed. She's living with him. I know a lot of young people live together these days, but I don't like it, living together and not married. It's not right.

He always makes such a noise! Listen! There he is now! Music! He's listening to music! Why can't he turn it down? It's so loud!

Young people these days have no manners, they live in their own world, and they just don't care about other people. They don't even notice old people like me. He probably doesn't know who I am.

T 2.11 **Two neighbours**

Alfie

I've got this new flat. It's so nice! I really love it. I'm having such a good time. The only thing is it's below an old lady, and that's a bit difficult. Her name's Mrs Crumble. I always say hello when I see her, 'How are you, Mrs Crumble?', 'Nice day, Mrs Crumble!' and all that, but she never replies. She just looks at me. I think she's deaf.

She probably thinks I'm unemployed because I don't go out to work in the morning and I don't wear a suit. I think I wear really cool clothes. Well, I'm a musician. I play the saxophone, and at the moment I'm playing in a jazz club. I don't start till 8.00 at night, and I don't finish till 2.00 in the morning, so I sleep from 3.00 till 11.00.

There's only me living here, but my flat's a bit busy at the moment because some of the other guys in the band are using it to keep their instruments in, so they're always coming in and out.

I've got a lovely girlfriend, she's the singer in the band. She's so beautiful! She lives the other side of town, but obviously I see her every day because we work together. She comes to my place sometimes. I know I make a bit of noise, because I practise my saxophone. See what I mean? What can I do? I have to practise somewhere!

I know that old Mrs Crumble is always watching me. It's sad because she has nothing to do. I feel sorry for her, and I'm always really kind to her like I am to my own grandmother, but she's so suspicious of young people. She thinks we're all no good and take drugs. It's just not true! I work really hard!

T 2.12 **Making conversation**

1: John and Maria

J   Hello. My name's John. What's your name?
M Maria.
J   Hi, Maria. Where are you from?
M Italy.
J   Ah, OK. Where in Italy are you from?
M Roma.
J   Ah, Rome. I love Rome. It's beautiful. And what do you do in Rome?
M I'm a student.
J   I see. And are you enjoying being in London?
M Yes.
J   Well, I've got a class now, Maria. Bye! See you again!
M Bye.
J   Not in my class, I hope.

2: Maggie and Jean-Jacques

M Hello. My name's Maggie. What's your name?
JJ My name is Jean-Jacques. Nice to meet you, Maggie.
M And you. Where are you from, Jean-Jacques?
JJ I'm French. I live in Paris – Paris, as you say in English – but I'm from the south, from Provence. Do you know the south of France?
M Yes, I do. It's beautiful!
JJ It's true! It is! And you, Maggie, where are you from?
M I'm from Scotland.
JJ Oh, really! I've never been there, but I'd like to. It's a beautiful country, isn't it?
M Very! Lots of mountains and lakes. What do you do in France, Jean-Jacques?
JJ I'm an architect. I design very expensive houses for very rich people.
M Wow! That's an interesting job! Are you enjoying being in London?

JJ Yes, I am. Very much. I'm having a really good time. I think London's really interesting city, and there's so much to do! And you, Maggie? What do you do?
M Well, I'm a teacher. I work here.
JJ Oh, really! What class are you teaching?
M 3B.
JJ Oh, great! That's my class! You're my teacher!
M Oh, how lovely! Well, it's 9.00. Let's go to class!
JJ What a good idea! I'll follow you …

T 2.13 **Making conversation**

1 A What a lovely day it is today!
   B Yes, beautiful, isn't it! Much nicer than yesterday.
2 A Are you having a good time in London?
   B Yes, I am. It's a very interesting city. There's so much to do. I love the shops.
3 A Have a good weekend!
   B Thanks. Same to you. Are you doing anything interesting?
4 A Did you have a nice weekend?
   B Yes, I did. It was really good. I saw some old friends. What did you do?
5 A What are you doing tonight?
   B Nothing special. Just at home. What about you?
6 A How's your mother these days?
   B She's OK, thanks. She's feeling a lot better. Thank you for asking.
7 A Did you watch the football last night?
   B No, I didn't. I missed it. Was it a good game?
8 A I like your shoes.
   B Thank you! They're new. I got them last week in the sales. They're nice, aren't they?
9 A If you have a problem, just ask me.
   B Thank you very much. That's very kind of you. I will.

T 2.14 **Keeping a conversation going**

A I was on holiday last month.
B Oh, really? Did you go away?
A Yes, I went to Italy.
B How wonderful! Italy's beautiful, isn't it?
A I think it's fabulous. I love all the history.
B Yes, and the buildings, and all the art! Where did you go?
A Well, first I went to Florence and I spent a few days going round the museums.
B Oh, fantastic! Did you see the statue of David?
A Oh, yes! Amazing! And then I went to see some friends who live in the countryside around Siena.
B Wow! Lucky you! Did you have good weather?
A Well, actually …

T 3.1 **Walking the Amazon**

Amazing journey ends after 6,000 miles

Ed Stafford became the first man in history to walk the length of the Amazon River from the source to the sea. He walked for 860 days. The journey began in April 2008 when Ed left the town of Camana on the Pacific coast of Peru. It ended in August 2010 when he arrived in Maruda, on the Atlantic coast of Brazil. He went through three countries, Peru, Colombia, and Brazil. The journey took nearly two and a half years. 'I did it for the adventure,' says Ed.

T 3.2 **Questions and answers**

1 A How far did Ed walk?
   B He walked six thousand miles.
2 A When did the journey begin?
   B It began in April 2008.
3 A Where did the journey end?
   B It ended in Maruda on the Atlantic coast of Brazil.
4 A Which countries did he go through?
   B He went through Peru, Colombia, and Brazil.
5 A How long did the journey take?
   B It took nearly two and a half years.
6 A Why did he do it?
   B He did it for the adventure.

T 3.3

A What was Cho doing when he met Ed?
B He was working in the forest.
A Where were they walking when they saw the tribe?
B They were walking in a very dangerous part of the forest.
A Why did the tribe think Ed was crazy?
B Because he was walking the Amazon for an adventure.

T 3.4 **Ed's blog**

12 July

The day I nearly died

Today I was walking next to the river when I nearly stood on a snake. I stopped immediately. The snake's fangs were going in and out. I was terrified. I didn't move. One bite and you're dead in three hours.

10 September

Knives and guns!

Early this morning we were crossing the river by boat when we saw five canoes. The tribesmen were carrying knives and guns. They were angry because we didn't have permission to be on their land. We left as fast as we could.

24 November

The jungle at night

I was lying in my hammock last night trying to sleep, but it was impossible because the noise of the jungle was so loud. Monkeys were screaming in the trees, and millions of mosquitos were buzzing round my head. I took a sleeping pill and finally fell asleep at 3.00 a.m.

T 3.5 Pronunciation /d/ /t/ /ɪd/

/d/ stayed, played, phoned, answered
/t/ stopped, worked, laughed, looked
/ɪd/ decided, studied, wanted, mended

T 3.6 Pronunciation

We stayed in a hotel.
They played on the beach.
She phoned a friend.
I answered all the questions.
They stopped at lunch time.
I worked in a bank.
We laughed and laughed.
I looked at the photo.
We decided immediately.
I studied at university.
She wanted a cup of tea.
I mended it.

T 3.7

I was having dinner.
What was she wearing?
They were playing football.
Where were you going?
He wasn't listening.
They weren't enjoying the party.

T 3.8 The news

Here are the news headlines.
A car bomb in Moscow kills three people.
Thieves steal paintings worth $80 million from a New York museum.
A national strike in France brings the country to a stop.
The 71-year-old actor James Robertson dies at his home in California.
And in the European Cup, Arsenal beat Real Madrid.

T 3.9

A car bomb exploded in central Moscow yesterday morning, killing three people who were shopping in a market and injuring many more. Most of those injured were women who were out shopping for food in the early morning, and children who were on holiday. Terrorists say they planted the bomb.
Last night thieves in New York broke into the Museum of Modern Art, and escaped with three paintings by Picasso, valued at $80 million. Cameras were recording the rooms all the time, but the guard who was watching the screens saw nothing. Museum officials didn't discover the theft until the next morning.
A national strike in France yesterday brought the country to a complete stop. Offices, banks, schools, and shops all closed, and there were no trains or buses throughout the whole country. Workers were protesting for higher pay, longer holidays, and a shorter working week.
The actor James Robertson died last night at his home in Hollywood, California. He was suffering from cancer. With him were his five children, his ex-wife, and his second wife, Cherie. The 71-year-old actor is best known for his role as the cowboy Dexter in *Mad Men of the West*.
And finally sport. Arsenal last night beat Real Madrid 2–1. At half-time the Spanish side were winning one nil, but then two goals by Johansson gave the London team a win.

T 3.10 A dictation

Last night thieves in New York broke into the Museum of Modern Art and escaped with three paintings by Picasso, valued at $80 million. Cameras were recording the rooms all the time, but the guard who was watching the screens saw nothing. Museum officials didn't discover the theft until the next morning.

T 3.11 Adverbs

1 Please drive carefully through our village.
2 Romeo loved Juliet passionately.
3 My mother speaks three languages fluently.
4 It rained heavily every day last week.
5 He waited patiently for his girlfriend, but she didn't turn up.
6 The soldiers fought bravely, but many of them lost their lives.

T 3.12 Word order

1 My grandma is nearly 75, and she still goes swimming regularly.
2 'Do you really love me?'
  'Of course I do. I'll always love you.'
3 I was just relaxing with a really good book when someone knocked loudly on the door.
4 My sister is only three, but she can already read, and she can write, too.
5 First, break the eggs into a bowl with some milk and butter. Then heat it gently. When it's ready, serve the scrambled eggs immediately with toast.
6 Almost all my friends have a mobile phone. They're on Facebook as well. Even my dad's on Facebook.

T 3.13 The burglar who fell asleep

Last Sunday evening, a burglar broke into a large, expensive house in the centre of Paris. First he went into the living room, and he quickly and quietly filled his sack with all the silverware and a priceless Chinese vase. Next he went to the kitchen and found some delicious cheese and two bottles of the best champagne. He was feeling extremely hungry and thirsty so he ate all the cheese and drank all the champagne. Suddenly he felt very tired. He went upstairs to the bedroom and lay down on a big, comfortable bed and immediately fell fast asleep. He slept very well. Unfortunately when he woke up the next morning, three policemen were standing round his bed.

T 3.14 Dates

A What's the date today?
B March the eighteenth. Tomorrow's the nineteenth. The day after tomorrow's the twentieth.
A When's your birthday?
B November the eighth.
A Oooh! That's next week.
A What's your date of birth?
B 12 – 9 – 87
A Sorry? What was that?
B The twelfth of the ninth, eighty-seven.
A What year were you born?
B 1982.
A Oh. You're the same age as me.

T 3.15

the third of February
February the third
the sixth of April
April the sixth
the twelfth of July
July the twelfth
the twenty-fifth of December
December the twenty-fifth
the first of May
May the first
the sixteenth of August
August the sixteenth
the thirteenth of January
January the thirteenth
the thirty-first of October
October the thirty-first

T 3.16

February third
April sixth
July twelfth
December twenty-fifth
May first
August sixteenth
January thirteenth
October thirty-first

T 3.17

1 A When did man first land on the moon?
  B On July the twentieth, 1969.
2 A When's your wedding anniversary?
  B November the eighth.
3 A When did the Berlin Wall come down?
  B The ninth of November, 1989.
4 A When was your son born?
  B July the twenty-first, 2010.
5 A What's the expiry date on your credit card?
  B 06 18

UNIT 4

T 4.1 Questions about the diet

1 Q Today we're talking to a couple who are following The Calorie Restriction Diet. So my first question is… Do you eat any meat?
  A No, we don't eat any meat at all, but we eat some fish.
2 Q How much fish do you eat?
  A We eat a little white fish, but we love shellfish so we eat a lot of prawns.
3 Q Do you eat much fruit?
  A Oh yes, we eat a lot of fresh fruit – apples and grapes – everything.
4 Q And do you eat many vegetables?
  A Yes, of course, we eat lots of raw vegetables.
5 Q Don't you cook any vegetables at all?
  A We cook some. Sometimes we steam a few carrots and a little broccoli.
6 Q And what do you drink?
  A Well, we don't drink any tea or coffee, and naturally there's no alcohol in our diet, but we do drink a lot of orange juice.
7 Q How many calories do you have every day?
  A About 1,500.
  A That's about 1,000 fewer than most people.

T 4.2 Following the diet

Q Tell us some more about the diet.
A Well, I think we have a good diet. We enjoy the food we do eat. For breakfast we have cereal, homemade cereal, we make it ourselves. We have it with fruit. We eat all fruit.
A But we don't eat any dairy products – no milk, no cheese and we don't eat bread so we don't need butter …
A We use olive oil instead. We often have it on salad for lunch with tomatoes and lots of nuts and sometimes green peppers stuffed with rice.
Q So you eat rice. What about pasta and potatoes?
A No, not at all. We don't eat anything made from potatoes.
Q No crisps or chips then. And I'm guessing you eat nothing made with sugar.
A You're right. We make fresh juice to drink, but with no sugar.
Q And nothing alcoholic of course. What about water?
A Well, we don't drink any tap water.
Q Really? Why not?
A It's not good for you. We drink a little mineral water sometimes.
Q You're amazing. Well, I hope you live to be 120, but I'm sure I won't be around to see it.

T 4.3 *something/someone/somewhere …*

1 A Did you meet anyone nice at the party?
  B Yes. I met somebody who knows you!
  A Oh, who was that?
  B Your ex-boyfriend.
2 A Ouch! There's something in my eye!
  B Let me look. No, I can't see anything.
  A But I can feel it. Somewhere in the corner of my eye.
3 A Let's go somewhere hot for our holidays.
  B But we can't go anywhere that's too expensive.
  A I know, but we can afford this package holiday to Turkey.

4 A Where are my glasses? I can't find them anywhere.
  B What are they on the top of your head?
  A My glasses! Thank you.
5 A It was a great party. Everybody loved it.
  B They did. Nobody wanted to go home.
  A I know. A few people were still dancing at 3.00 a.m.
6 A Did you get anything nice in the sales?
  B No, nothing. I couldn't find anything I liked.
  A Why not try shopping online? You can buy everything online these days.

T 4.4 What's the missing word?

Do you know … famous?
The fridge is empty. There's … to eat!
The lights are off. There's … at home.
Pete's a great bloke. … likes him.
We always go … nice to eat.
I can't go to the party. I haven't got … nice to wear!
Has … seen my keys?
I can't find my keys …

T 4.5 My grandfather's shop

My grandfather lived until he was 101 years old. He was a shopkeeper. He had a fish and chip shop in an old village near a big, industrial town in the north of England. He had a son and a daughter. The daughter is my mother. The family lived above the shop.
In those days, fish and chips was the most popular dish in the whole country. My grandfather made the best fish and chips in the area. People came to the village by bus especially to get them. Everybody loved my grandfather because he was such a happy and contented man. He worked hard, but once a week he closed the shop and went to have lunch (not fish and chips!) with friends in the local pub. He didn't retire until he was 78 years old. He said that the secret to a long life was a glass of whisky before going to bed and lots of fish and chips.

T 4.6 Articles

My grandfather was a shopkeeper
He lived in the north of England.
He had a fish and chip shop in an old village.
His family lived above the shop.
He made the best fish and chips in the area.
Some people came by bus to the shop.
He closed the shop once a week.
He went to have lunch with friends.
He liked to have a little whisky before bed.

T 4.7 Unusual restaurants

1 Alexander

We were on honeymoon and we saw some brochures about this restaurant. It was my wife's birthday so I thought why not – it's expensive, but you don't find many restaurants like this. It was difficult to get a reservation because it only takes twelve people. When we arrived we had drinks on the deck above and someone gave us a talk about how they built the restaurant and then we took off our shoes and descended, – down, down the spiral stairs and into the restaurant. Actually, the restaurant itself isn't very exciting, the decor I mean, but it doesn't need to be because what is totally amazing is the view – it takes your breath away. All around and above your head are hundreds, maybe thousands, of fish, all colours in a blue, blue sea. I was sitting opposite my wife when a turtle appeared just behind her head. In

fact we were so busy looking at it all we almost forgot that we were there to eat. The food was delicious, fish of course, but to be honest we felt a bit bad eating white fish, surrounded by white fish. There was just one problem, a guest at the next table. He spoke really loudly and complained about everything. We couldn't find anything to complain about. It was the perfect honeymoon restaurant.

2 Hans

I booked online of course. It's the only way you can book. And I went with my sons – they are five and eight years old – and I thought they would like it a lot. They were very excited. They had the idea that the waiters were robots, so when we arrived and there was nobody there at all they were a bit disappointed. But the whole place was amazing. It was like walking inside a computer, so the boys soon became excited again. We picked up a card and sat down at one of the big round, red tables. The boys loved the touch-screen TVs. They got the idea immediately and started choosing food from the pictures. While we were waiting they were texting their mother to tell her how fantastic it all was. In just a few minutes pots with our meals inside came flying down the spiral tubing in the middle of the table. The boys couldn't believe it, they were shouting with excitement. We all had steak and salad and then the boys had baked bananas with ice cream and chocolate. It was delicious. There was an older lady sitting next to us. She was a bit confused so we helped her. She said, 'I think this is more for young people than people my age'. Maybe she's right.

3 Lucy

I was hungry when I arrived at the restaurant, but when I saw the crane I forgot about being hungry. I was so frightened. The host, David, said 'Don't worry, it's 100% safe'. Huh! I'm sure a few of the other guests felt like me – they looked very pale. Anyway, we sat down at this huge table, fastened our seat belts and up, up, up we went.
I couldn't look down. Everyone was saying, 'What a wonderful view', but I just couldn't look. Then one of the waiters put a glass of wine in my hand and I opened my eyes and the view was amazing. People were waving to us from the ground. They probably thought we were mad. The weather was perfect, thank goodness, just a little breeze. I began to enjoy it. The other guests were all great fun. I didn't know anyone at the start, but I soon made some friends and the food was good too, especially the prawns. The chef cooked them in front of us on a tiny cooker. But best of all, was at the end, when everybody learnt my name they started singing 'Lucy in the sky with diamonds'. No diamonds, but I was certainly in the sky. I was quite sorry when we came down to earth again.

T 4.8

a piece of paper
a loaf of bread
a bottle of beer
a can of Coke
a kilo of apples
a litre of petrol
a packet of chewing gum
a pair of jeans
a slice of cake
a bunch of bananas

T 4.9 **Going shopping**

1 A Just this copy of *The Times*, please.
   B That's £1 exactly.
   A Sorry, I only have a £20 note.
   B No problem. I've got change.
   A Thanks. Oh, and can I have a packet of chewing gum as well?
   B OK. That's £1.79 now, please.
2 A Excuse me, how much is this pair of socks?
   B They're £4.60 a pair.
   A OK. Can I have two pairs, please? Have you got any in blue?
   B I'm afraid they only come in grey and black.
   A Never mind. A black and a grey pair, please.
   B That's £9.20 altogether. How would you like to pay?
3 A Good morning. Can we have two double espressos, and a latte, please?
   B What size latte?
   A Just medium, please. Oh, and three slices of chocolate cake. It looks delicious.
   B I'm afraid there are only two slices left, but the carrot cake's good too.
   A OK. And one slice of carrot cake, then.
   B Certainly. That's £11.80.
4 A Can you help me? I need something for a very bad cold.
   B Yes, of course. Are you allergic to aspirin?
   A No, I'm not.
   B OK. Take these three times a day.
   A Thank you.
   B Do you want a bottle or a pack?
   A I don't mind. A bottle's fine. And can I have two packets of tissues as well, please?
   B Sure. Anything else?
   A No, that's all. How much is that?
   B That's £5.40 altogether.
5 A Five cans of beer and four packets of crisps, please.
   B How old are you?
   A Er … I'm eighteen.
   B Well, you don't look eighteen.
   C He is eighteen.
   B And you look about twelve! Have you got any ID?
   A Not with me, I haven't.
   B Then I can't sell you the beer.
   A Oh, OK, just the packets of crisps then and two cans of Coke.
6 A Good morning. What can I get for you?
   B Er- three, no, make that four slices of ham, please. Organic ham.
   A OK. That's -er four slices. Anything else?
   B Yes, can I have that large piece of cheese?
   A The Cheddar?
   B That's right. How much is that?
   A £8.35. But you don't pay here. You pay at the checkout with your other goods.
   B Oh, OK. And can you tell me where the fruit and veg are?
   A They're on the first aisle, over there.
   B Oh, thanks very much. I'm lost in this place. It's my first time and it's huge.

T 4.10 **Friends for dinner**

1 A Would you like some more rice?
   B No, thanks. But could I have another piece of bread?
   A Of course. Do you want white or brown?
2 A Could you pass the salt, please?
   B Yes, of course. Do you want the pepper too?
   A No, thanks. Just the salt.
3 A Can I have some water, please?
   B Do you want still or sparkling?
   A Just a glass of tap water is fine, thank you.
4 A Please, just help yourselves to the dessert.
   B We will. It looks fantastic. Did you make it yourself?
   A I did. It's my grandmother's recipe.
5 A Would anybody like some more ice cream?
   B No, but I'd love some more fruit. Is there any left?
   A There is a bit. It's all yours.
6 A How would you like your coffee?
   B Black, no sugar. Have you got any decaf?
   A No, sorry. I'm afraid not, but we've got decaf tea. Would that be OK?
7 A This is delicious! Would you mind giving me the recipe?
   B No, not at all. I got it online. I'll give you the website.
   A Thanks. I get lots of my recipes online too.
8 A Do you want some help with the washing-up?
   B No, of course not. You're our guests!
   A Well, I hope you have a dishwasher. There's a lot.

T 4.11 **Polite requests with *can* and *could***

1 A Can I have some apple juice, please?
   B Sorry, we haven't got any apple juice. Will orange juice do?
2 A Could you tell me where Market Street is, please?
   B Sorry, I'm afraid I'm a stranger here myself.
3 A Can I see the menu, please?
   B Here you are. Today's specials are on the board over there.
4 A Could I use your iPad for a few minutes, please?
   B Eva's using it at the moment. But you can have it after her.
5 A Could you lend me £20, please?
   B Mmm … I can lend you ten, but not twenty.
6 A Can you take me to school, please?
   B Goodness, is that the time? We're going to be late!
7 A Can you help me with my homework, please?
   B OK, but I'm not very good at maths.
8 A Could you give me a lift to the station, please?
   B Of course. What time's your train?

T 4.12 **Polite requests with *Would you mind …?***

A Would you mind lending me £20? I'll pay you back tomorrow.
B No, not at all. Is twenty enough?
A Would you mind taking me to school, please? I missed the bus.
B Not again! That's the third time this week!
A Would you mind helping me with my homework? I have no idea how to do it.
B I don't mind helping you, but I'm not doing it for you.
A Would you mind giving me a lift to the station? I've got a lot of heavy bags to carry.
B Not at all. Are you ready to go now?

UNIT 5

T 5.1 **Verb patterns**

Tom

I'm sixteen and I'm fed up with school and exams. I'd like to leave now and get a job, any job. I want to earn some money, but my mum and dad say that I can't leave school. They think I'll regret it later, but I don't think I will.

Abby

I'm a student in my last year at university. I've got debts of nearly £25,000. I'm going to study hard for my exams because I hope to get a well-paid job. I hate owing so much money. I'm going for an interview next Friday. Wish me luck!

Kelly

I'm a paramedic. I love my job, but it's very stressful. I'm looking forward to having a good break. We're going to Spain this summer. I'm planning to do nothing but read on the beach for two whole weeks!

Martin

I work in IT. There's nothing I don't know about computers, but I need a change. I'm thinking of applying for another job with a company in New York. I saw it advertised online and it looks like the job for me. I'd love to work there for a couple of years.

Alison

I've got three kids under seven and my husband works abroad a lot of the time. I enjoy looking after the kids, but I'd love to travel too. Sometimes I get fed up with staying at home all day. I'm looking forward to going back to work in a year or two.

Bill

I'm a retired newsagent and I didn't have a day off for 40 years. Now I like sleeping late and planning holidays on the Internet for me and my wife. I'm pretty good at using a computer. We're going on holiday to Tuscany next year so I'm going to do an evening course in Italian.

T 5.2

1 I want to work in Paris.
   I'd like to work in Paris.
2 We like going to Italy for our holidays.
   We're thinking of going to Italy for our holidays.
3 She can't leave work early tonight.
4 I hope to see you again soon.
   I'd like to see you again soon.
5 He's good at playing sports games on the Wii.
   He enjoys playing sports games on the Wii.
6 Are you good at learning foreign languages?
7 We're looking forward to having a few days off soon.
8 I'm fed up with doing housework.
   I hate doing housework.

1 I enjoy working in Paris.
2 We're hoping to go to Italy for our holidays.
3 She wants to leave work early tonight.
  She'd like to leave work early tonight.
4 I'm looking forward to seeing you again soon.
5 He wants to play sports games on the Wii.
6 Do you want to learn foreign languages?
  Do you like learning foreign languages?
7 We're going to have a few days off soon.
  We'd love to have a few days off soon.
8 I don't want to do housework.

T 5.4 **Making questions**

1 A I hope to go to university.
  B What do you want to study?
  A I'm going to study philosophy and politics.
     I'd like to be prime minister.
  B I think that's the worst job in the world!
2 A One of my favourite hobbies is cooking.
  B What do you like making?
  A Well, I love baking cakes, all kinds of cakes.
  B OK, can I have a huge chocolate cake for
     my birthday?
3 A I'm bored.
  B What would you like to do?
  A Nothing. I'm happy being bored.
  B Well, that's OK then!
4 A I'm looking forward to the party.
  B Who are you hoping to see there?
  A No one special. I just like parties.
  B Me too!
5 A We're planning our summer holidays.
  B Where are you thinking of going?
  A We want to go camping this year.
  B Ugh! Camping! I hate sleeping in tents.

T 5.5 **Writing for talking**
My dreams for the future

Hello everyone. My name's Susannah – Susie for
short. I'm 20 years old. At the moment I'm in my
second year at art school and I often dream about
my future. I have big plans and I'd like to tell you a
bit about them.
My most immediate plans are holiday plans.
I'm going to visit my brother who's working in
Australia. My mother and I are going to spend
Christmas with him in the summer sun. I'm very
excited about that.
When I return I need to make a final decision
about which course to study next year. I'm still
not sure – I'm thinking of doing either fashion
design or landscape design. It's difficult because
I'm interested in both clothes and gardens. If I
choose landscape I'd like to work with my friend
Jasper. He's brilliant with gardens and we've
already worked on two together. It was great fun
and we get on very well.
In five or ten years' time I would like to have my
own business and work for myself like my father.
He has his own building business. Perhaps I'll do
a business course after I finish art school.
Of course, one day I hope to marry and have
children. Ideally before I'm 30, but I can't plan
when I'll meet the right person and I haven't got a
boyfriend at the moment.
In my dreams I see myself at 40 running a
successful gardening company with about 20
employees. I'll design beautiful gardens for
beautiful people. I'll have a beautiful house, two
beautiful children, and of course a husband who's
as successful as I am. Who knows, it could even
be Jasper!

T 5.6 **Have you got any plans?**
1 **Pete and Ben**
B Hi Pete! What are you doing this evening?
P Hi Ben. I'm meeting my brother for a drink.
   Would you like to come?
B Sorry I can't. I'm working late this evening.
   But … are you doing anything interesting this
   weekend?
P Yes, I am. I'm going to stay with an old school
   friend. It's his birthday and he's having a party.
B Are you going to have a party for your
   birthday?
P Of course! I'm going to invite all my friends.
B Great! I'll look forward to that! Hey, where are
   you going on holiday this year?
P I'm going surfing for two weeks in Costa Rica.
   I'm really excited.
B Wow, that sounds fantastic. I'm not going
   anywhere this year. I can't afford it.
P Yeah, but that's 'cos you're saving to buy a flat.
B I know. You can't have everything. Give my
   best to your brother. I'll see you later.

2 **Debbie and Ella**
E Hey Debbie! It's the weekend. Are you doing
   anything interesting?
D No, I'm not. I'll give you a ring and maybe we
   can do something together.
E Sorry, I can't this weekend. I'm going on
   holiday on Saturday.
D Oh, lucky you! Where to?
E Greece, for a week. Where are you going
   this year?
D Oh, I can't decide. Perhaps I'll go cycling in
   France again. Hey, are you back from holiday
   for my birthday on the 25th?
E Yes, I am. Are you going to have a party?
D I haven't thought about it. Maybe I'll just
   celebrate at home with a few friends.
E Nice idea! So what about tonight? What are
   you doing this evening?
D Nothing much. I think I'll just watch a DVD
   and order a pizza. Hey, why don't you come
   round and join me?
E OK, I'll do that, but I won't stay late. My plane
   leaves at eight in the morning.

T 5.7 **Discussing grammar**
1 A Have you decided which university to
     apply for?
  B Oh yes, I'm going to apply for Oxford.
  A Good luck! That's difficult to get into.
2 A I haven't got your mobile number.
  B Really? I'll text it to you right now.
  A Thanks. Do you have mine?
  B Yes, I think so.
3 A We don't have any fruit in the house.
  B I'm going shopping this afternoon. I'll get
     some apples.
  A Great. I'll give you the money for them.
4 A My bag is really heavy.
  B Give it to me. I'll carry it for you.
  A Thanks.
  B My goodness. What have you got in here?
5 A Tony's back from holiday.
  B Is he? I'll give him a ring.
  A I'm seeing him this evening. Do you want
     to come?
6 A What are we having for supper?
  B I'm going to make spaghetti bolognese.
  A Not again! We had that twice last week.

T 5.8 **What can you say?**
1 Why are you looking forward to the weekend?
2 I haven't got your brother's new address.
3 Mary says she hasn't seen you for months.
4 Why are you dressed in old clothes?
5 Congratulations! I hear you've got a new job.
6 Are you doing anything interesting after class?

T 5.9 **What can you say?**
1 A Why are you looking forward to the
     weekend?
  B Because I'm going to the theatre with friends.
2 A I haven't got your brother's new address.
  B Haven't you? I'll give it to you now.
3 A Mary says she hasn't seen you for months.
  B I know. I'll call her this evening.
4 A Why are you dressed in old clothes?
  B Because I'm going to help my dad in the
     garden.
5 A Congratulations! I hear you've got a
     new job.
  B Yes, I'm going to work in New York.
6 A Are you doing anything interesting after
     class?
  B No, I'm not. I'm just going home.

T 5.10 *Will you, won't you?*
1 I think you'll pass your driving test. You won't
  fail again. It's your fourth time.
2 I think my team will win. They won't lose this
  time. They've got a new manager.
3 I think it'll be warm today. You won't need
  your jumper. Just take a T-shirt.
4 I think I'll join a gym. I won't go on a diet.
  I like my food too much.
5 I think they'll get divorced. They won't stay
  together. They argue all the time.
6 I think I'll go by train. I won't fly. I hate flying.

T 5.11 The 20-somethings!

Leo, aged 28

I had a real shock the other day. My little nephew, he's six, said to me 'Uncle Leo, when you were a little boy did they have telephones?' I couldn't believe it. I said: 'Of course we had telephones. How old do you think I am?' Then he said: 'But did you have mobile phones?' And I thought, 'did we?' I can't remember life without mobile phones, but in fact …-er I think I was about eight when my dad got one. 'Yeah,' I said, 'When I was eight'. 'Aha!' said my nephew 'I knew it. You are old'. I didn't like hearing that! I'm 28 and I don't feel grown up at all. I have a great life – a good job, lots of friends, I go out with them most nights. I go to the gym every morning. I'm going to buy a flat by the river next year. Maybe when I'm in my 30s I'll get married and start a family.

Elsa, aged 26

I finished university and I started training to be a lawyer. I was earning good money and in many ways I had a good life but -er the more I studied law the more I hated it, I was bored and miserable – so I decided to give it all up and go travelling. I was away for a year. I went to Australia, New Zealand, North and South America – it was fantastic, but then I arrived back home. I was now 24 and with no money, no job, and nowhere to live. I moved back with mum and dad – they're wonderful, they don't make me pay rent, but – oh dear – it's like being a little girl again. At the moment I'm working as a waitress just to make a bit of money and my dad keeps asking 'When are you going to find a real job?', and mum says: 'When I was your age I was married with two children.' Married with kids! I don't feel old enough for that! I've got a boyfriend but we're not thinking of getting married. Maybe I'll train to be a teacher, now that's a real job.

Dan, aged 24

When I left home at 18 I thought that was it – 'Goodbye mum and dad'. Now six years later I'm back! My college days were great – I worked hard and played hard but I left with huge debts – over £15,000. I thought, 'No problem, I'll just get a job and pay it back'. I moved into a flat with some friends and I was lucky – I got a job pretty quickly, but … I want to be a journalist and the only way is to begin at the bottom. I'm a very junior reporter for a small local newspaper. I love working there, but I only earn £16,000 a year. I couldn't afford the rent for the flat, so here I am, back with mum and dad. They call us the 'boomerang kids' – you know, kids who grow up, leave home, and then move back again. Lots of my friends are doing the same, my girlfriend is back with her mum too. One day we're hoping to marry and get a place of our own, but that probably won't be for a few years. You can't grow up when you're still at home with your parents. I'm fed up.

T 5.12 An interview with Palina Yanachkina

I = Interviewer, P = Palina

I Today I'm talking to Palina Yanachkina. Palina, it's nice to meet you. Can I ask you some questions?

P Of course.

I I hear that you call yourself the girl with two families. Why is that?

P Well, I have my family back home in the Ukraine and my family here in Ireland.

I Where exactly do you come from?

P I come from the village of Polessye not far from Chernobyl. I was born in 1988 just two years after the nuclear accident there. It was a terrible time for us.

I I can understand that. What happened to your family?

P My parents are farmers and after the accident they couldn't sell any of their produce. No one wanted to buy our meat or vegetables. We were very poor and ill – like many people in the village.

I How awful, how miserable for you all.

P But I was lucky. I had the chance to go to Ireland for a holiday and that was when I met my second family. I loved staying with them, -er they were so kind to me. They looked after me so well.

I Your English is excellent now. Did you speak English then?

P Not a word. But I soon learnt, especially from the children. I got on really well with them.

I So you picked up English bit by bit?

P I had some lessons too and I came back to Ireland many times.

I What are you doing now?

P I'm studying here in Ireland. My wonderful Irish family are paying for my studies. I'm hoping to become a doctor one day and return to my village to help the people there. That's my big hope for the future.

I Well, I'm sure you'll do that one day. Thank you, Palina. I've enjoyed talking to you.

T 5.13 Talking about you

1 Where did you grow up? Do you still live in the same house?
2 How do you get on with your parents?
3 Do you ever fall out with your friends and stop speaking to them?
4 Would you like to be a doctor or nurse and look after people?
5 Are you good at picking up foreign languages?
6 Do you look up lots of words in your dictionary?

T 5.14 Expressing doubt and certainty

1 A Do you think Tom will pass his exams?
  B I doubt it. He's fed up with school.
  C I know. He has no chance at all. He wants to leave and get a job.
2 A Does Martin earn a lot of money?
  B Yes, absolutely. He earns a fortune.
  C Mmm … I'm not sure. He wants to change his job.
3 A Are England going to win the World Cup?
  B They might do. Anything's possible, but I think it's very unlikely.
  A Absolutely! I don't think they have a chance.

T 5.15

1 A Kelly's job is really stressful, isn't it?
  B Absolutely. She's a paramedic.
  A Is she having a holiday soon?
  B I think so. She says she might go to Spain.
2 A Isn't it Rob's birthday next week?
  B Yes, definitely. It's on the 21st.
  A So he's a Capricorn.
  B No, I don't think so. I think he's an Aquarius.
3 A Do you think Anita and Paul are in love?
  B Definitely. They're going to get married next June in Hawaii.
  A Hawaii! Are you going to the wedding?
  B No chance. I can't afford it.

T 5.16 What's your opinion?

1 A Did Leo Tolstoy write *War and Peace*?
  B Definitely. He wrote it in 1869.
2 A Is Nicole Kidman American?
  B I don't think so. I think she's Australian.
3 A Was Sherlock Holmes a real person?
  B Definitely not. He's from a book by a writer called Conan Doyle.
4 A Is the population of China more than 2 billion?
  B It might be. I don't know. It's definitely more than 1 billion.
5 A Do some vegetarians eat fish?
  B I think so. I have a friend who's vegetarian and she eats fish.
6 A Is the weather going to be nice next weekend?
  B I doubt it. It's cold and wet today.
7 A Are you going to be rich and famous one day?
  B No chance. I'd like to be a bit richer than now, but I wouldn't like to be famous.
8 A Is your school the best in town?
  B Absolutely. It's definitely the best.

UNIT 6

T 6.1 **Questions about Mia**
1 A Do you like Mia?
   B Yes, I do. I like her a lot.
2 A How's Mia?
   B She's fine, thanks. Very well.
3 A What's Mia like?
   B She's really nice. Very friendly.
4 A What does Mia look like?
   B She's tall, and she's got brown eyes and
      black hair.

T 6.2
1 A What's your teacher like?
   B She's great! She helps us a lot.
2 A What sports do you like?
   B Cycling and skiing.
3 A What does your brother look like?
   B He's got blond hair and blue eyes.
4 A Do you like pizza?
   B Mmm, I love it!
5 A What's the weather like today?
   B Lovely! Warm and sunny.
6 A How are your parents?
   B They're OK. Busy as usual.

T 6.3 **What's it like?**
T What's Shanghai like?
M It's very big and noisy, but it's very exciting.
T What's the food like?
M It's the best in the world! I just love Chinese
   food!
T What are the people like?
M They're very friendly, and they really want to
   do business.
T What was the weather like?
M When I was there, it was hot and humid.
T What are the buildings like?
M There are new buildings everywhere, but if
   you look hard, you can still find some older
   ones, too.

T 6.4 **Singapore, Shanghai, and Dubai**
T What did you think of Singapore? What's it like?
M Well, Singapore is very old. It's older than
   Shanghai, but it's a lot smaller. Shanghai has a
   population of 20 million, and it's enormous!
   Shanghai is much bigger than Singapore, and
   it's much noisier, too.
T Oh, OK. What about business? What's it like to
   do business in these places?
M Well, they're both top financial centres, but
   Singapore is more important. It's better for
   investment.
T Ah, right. And the buildings? Are they all new?
M Yeah, there are a lot of new buildings in
   Shanghai, so it's more modern than Singapore,
   but it isn't as cosmopolitan. Half the
   population of Singapore are foreigners.
T Wow! Really? What about Dubai? What's
   that like?
M Dubai is the newest and youngest city, and it's
   the most modern. I like it because it has a 'can-
   do' feel to it.
T What about the climate in these places? What
   was the weather like?
M It's interesting. Singapore is very near the
   equator, so it's a lot hotter than Shanghai. But
   it isn't as hot as Dubai. Dubai is the hottest
   place. When I was there the temperature was
   over 40 degrees.

T Wow! That's incredible!
M Singapore is very humid, so it's wetter than
   Shanghai. But Dubai is the driest. It only rains
   for a few days a year.
T Where did you like most of all? Where was
   best for you?
M For me Shanghai is the best because it's the
   busiest and the most exciting. There are so
   many things to do – the best restaurants,
   theatres, shops. It's got everything!

T 6.5 **Pronunciation**
I'm older than Jane.
But I'm not as old as John.
He's the oldest.

T 6.6 **Ben and me**
A Who's cleverer, you or Ben?
B *Me*, of course! I'm *much* cleverer than Ben.
   He isn't nearly as clever as me!

T 6.7
A Who's kinder, you or Ben?
B *Me*, of course! I'm *much* kinder than Ben.
   He isn't nearly as kind as me!
A Who's funnier, you or Ben?
B *Me*, of course! I'm *much* funnier than Ben.
   He isn't nearly as funny as me!
A Who's better-looking, you or Ben?
B *Me*, of course! I'm *a lot* better looking than
   Ben. He isn't nearly as good looking as me!
A Who's more ambitious, you or Ben?
B *Me*, of course! I'm *much* more ambitious than
   Ben. He isn't nearly as ambitious as me!

T 6.8 **Me and my family**
Sally
Well, I'm very like my mum. We're interested in
the same kind of things, and we can talk forever.
We like the same films and the same books. I
look like my mum, too. We have the same hair,
the same eyes. And she's the same size as me, so I
can wear her clothes! My sister's a bit older than
me. Her name's Lena. We're quite different. She's
very tidy, and I'm messy. She's much tidier than
me. And she's very ambitious. She wants to be a
doctor. I'm a lot lazier. I don't know what I want
to do.

Jamie
I'm not really like my mum or my dad, but I'm a
twin. I've got a twin brother called Rob, and we
look a lot like each other. He's just a bit darker
than me. I've got blonder hair. His is more kind
of fair.
But people are always mixing us up. People come
up to me and say hello and start a conversation,
and I have no idea who they are. It's quite funny.
I just say 'Yeah!' or 'Really?' We're very similar in
character. We both love art and theatre and books,
but he's a bit moody and quiet. I'm a lot noisier.
I guess he's quite shy. Oh, and I'm definitely
cleverer than him!

Rachel
People say I'm like my father. Hmm. Not sure
about that. We do look the same. We're both
quite tall, and I suppose our faces are similar. But
my father's a very selfish man, and I hope I'm
different from him. I hope I'm a bit kinder. He
doesn't talk much. He isn't very cheerful. I'm a
lot happier than him. He doesn't sound very nice,
does he? He's OK, but there are things about him
that I really don't like. I have a sister, Jenny, and
we do everything together. I love her to bits. But
she's prettier than me and thinner than me, so I
hate her!

T 6.9 **Synonyms**
1 A Jane comes from a very rich family.
   B Really? I knew her uncle was very wealthy.
      They have a house in the south of France,
      don't they?
2 A Was Sophie angry when you were late?
   B Yeah. She was pretty annoyed, it's true. She
      shouted for a bit, then she calmed down.
3 A Jack's such an intelligent boy!
   B Mm. He's very clever for a ten-year old. He
      has some interesting things to say, as well.
4 A I've had enough of winter now.
   B I know. I'm fed up with all these dark
      nights. I need some sunshine.
5 A Dave and Sarah's flat is small, isn't it?
   B Mm. It's tiny. I don't know how they live
      there. It's only big enough for one person.
6 A Are you happy with your new car?
   B Yes, I'm very pleased with it. It goes really
      well. And it's much more reliable than my
      old one.

T 6.10 **Antonyms**
1 A That man was so rude to me!
   B Yes, he wasn't very polite, was he?
2 A Some people are so stupid!
   B Well, not everyone's as clever as you!
3 A Dave's flat is always so dirty!
   B Mm, it isn't very clean, is it?
4 A His wife always looks so miserable!
   B Yeah, she never looks very happy, does she?
5 A Their children are so naughty!
   B Yes, they aren't very well-behaved, are they?
6 A This lesson is boring!
   B True. It isn't very interesting. I can't wait for
      it to end.

T 6.11 **What's on?**
1 A What shall we do today?
   B I'm not sure. How about going to the
      cinema?
   A Mmm … I don't really feel like seeing a film.
2 B OK. Would you like to go to an exhibition?
   A That sounds interesting! What's on?
   B Well, there's a Van Gogh exhibition.
   A Is it any good?
   B I think it looks really good!
3 A Where is it on?
   B It's on at the Royal Academy.
   A What's the nearest underground?
   B Piccadilly Circus.
   A How much is it?
   B It's £12, and £8 for students.
   A What time is it open?
   B From ten till six.
   A Right! Good idea! Let's go!

Grammar Reference

UNIT 1

 ### 1.1 Tenses

This unit has examples of the Present Simple and Present Continuous, the Past Simple, and two future forms: *going to* and the Present Continuous for the future.

All these tenses are covered again in later units.

Present tenses   Unit 2
Past tenses   Units 3 and 9
Future forms   Unit 5

The aim in this unit is to revise what you already know.

Present tenses
She **lives** in London.
I **earn** $100 a day.
I'm **saving** money for my education.
They're **studying** in a language school.

Past tense
They **moved** to Canada thirty years ago.
I **had** a bad accident last month.

Future forms
I'm **going to** study for a Master's degree.
What **are you doing** tonight?

 ### 1.2 Auxiliary verbs

The Present Continuous uses the auxiliary verb *to be* in all forms.

Positive	**Question**
She **is** reading.	**Is** she reading?
They **are** watching a film.	What **are** they watching?

Negative
He **isn't** learning French.
I'm **not** sleeping.

Verb forms with no auxiliary verb
In the Present Simple and the Past Simple there is no auxiliary verb in the positive. We use the auxiliary verb *do* in the questions and negatives.

Positive	**Question**
They live in Australia.	**Do** they live in London?
He arrived yesterday.	Where **did** Bill go?

Negative
I **don't** work in New York.
We **didn't** watch TV.

1.3 Questions

1   *Yes/No* questions have no question word.
   Are you hot?   Yes, I am./No, I'm not.
   Does he speak English?   Yes, he does./No, he doesn't.

2   Questions can begin with a question word.

what	where	which	how	who	when	why	whose

   Where's the station?
   Why are you laughing?
   Whose is this coat?
   How does she go to work?

3   *What*, *which*, and *whose* can be followed by a noun.
   What size do you take?
   Which coat is yours?
   Whose book is this?

4   *Which* is generally used when there is a limited choice.
   Which is your pen? The black one or the blue one?

   This rule is not always true.

   What
   Which | newspaper do you read?

5   *How* can be followed by an adjective or an adverb.
   How big is his new car?
   How fast does it go?

   How can also be followed by *much* or *many*.
   How much is this sandwich?
   How many brothers and sisters have you got?

2.1 Present Simple

Form

Positive and negative

I You We They	live don't live	near here.
He She It	lives doesn't live	

Question

Where	do	I you we they	live?
	does	he she it	

	Short answer
Do you like Peter?	*Yes*, *I* **do.**
Does he speak French?	*No*, *he* **doesn't.**

Use

The Present Simple is used to express:

1 a habit.
   I **get up** *at 7.30.*
   Jo **smokes** *too much.*

2 a fact which is always true.
   Vegetarians **don't eat** *meat.*
   We **come** *from Spain.*

3 a fact which is true for a long time.
   I **live** *in Oxford.*
   She **works** *in a bank.*

 2.2 Present Continuous

Form

am/is/are + *-ing* (present participle)

Positive and negative

I	'm (am) 'm not	
He She It	's (is) isn't	working.
You We They	're (are) aren't	

Question

What	am	I	wearing?
	is	he she it	
	are	you we they	

	Short answer	
Are you going?	*Yes*, *I* **am.**/*No*, *I'm* **not.**	NOT ~~*Yes, I'm.*~~
Is Anna working?	*Yes*, *she* **is.**/*No*, *she* **isn't.**	NOT ~~*Yes, she's.*~~

Use

The Present Continuous is used to express:

1 an activity happening now.
   They **'re playing** *football in the garden.*
   She can't talk now because she's **washing** *her hair.*

2 an activity happening around now, but perhaps not at the moment of speaking.
   He's **studying** *maths at university.*
   I'm **reading** *a good book at the moment.*

3 a planned future arrangement.
   I'm **seeing** *the doctor at 10.00 tomorrow.*
   What **are** *you* **doing** *this evening?*

 2.3 Present Simple and Present Continuous

1 Read the right and wrong sentences.
   Fraser **comes** *from Scotland.*
   NOT ~~*Fraser is coming from Scotland.*~~
   I'm **reading** *a good book at the moment.*
   NOT ~~*I read a good book at the moment.*~~

2 Some verbs express a state, not an activity, and are usually used in the Present Simple only.
   She **likes** *the Rolling Stones.*
   NOT ~~*She's liking the Rolling Stones.*~~
   I **know** *what you mean.*
   NOT ~~*I'm knowing what you mean.*~~
   Similar verbs are *think, agree, understand, love.*

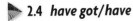

2.4 *have got/have*

Form

Positive

I/You/We/They	have 've got	two sisters.
He/She	has 's got	

Negative

I/You/We/They	don't have haven't got	any money.
He/She	doesn't have hasn't got	

Question

Do	I/you/we/they	have	a new car?
Does	he/she		
Have	I/you/we/they	got	a new car?
Has	he/she		

Short answer

Do you have an iPhone?	**Yes, I do./No, I don't.**
Have you got an iPhone?	**Yes, I have./No, I haven't.**

Note

We can use contractions (*'ve* and *'s*) with *have got*, but not with *have*.
***I've got** a sister.*
***I have** a sister.* NOT ~~*I've a sister.*~~

Use

1 *Have* and *have got* mean the same. *Have got* is more informal.
   We use it a lot when we speak, but not so much when we write.
   ***Have** you **got** the time?*
   *The UK **has** a population of 60 million.*

   In American English, *have + do/does* is much more common.

2 *Have* and *have got* express possession.

I have I've got	a new car.
She has She's got	three children.
He has He's got	blond hair.

3 When *have* + noun expresses an activity or a habit, *have* (not *have got*) is used. Look at these sentences.
   *I **have** a shower every day.*
   NOT ~~*I've got a shower every day.*~~

   *What time do you **have** lunch?*
   NOT ~~*What time have you got lunch?*~~

4 In the past tense, we use *had* with *did* and *didn't*.
   *I **had** a bicycle when I was young.*
   ***Did** you **have** a nice weekend?*
   *I **didn't have** any money when I was a student.*

3.1 Past Simple

Form

The form of the Past Simple is the same for all persons.

Positive

I He/She/It You We They	finished arrived went	yesterday.

Negative

The negative of the Past Simple is formed with *didn't*.

I He/She/It You We They	didn't (did not) arrive	yesterday.

Question

The question in the Past Simple is formed with *did*.

When	did	she/you/they/etc.	arrive?

	Short answer
Did you go to work yesterday?	***Yes, I did.***
Did it rain last night?	***No, it didn't.***

Spelling of regular verbs

1 The normal rule is to add *-ed* or *-d*.
work/work**ed**   start/start**ed**   live/liv**ed**   love/lov**ed**

2 Some short verbs with only one syllable double the consonant.
stop/sto**pp**ed   plan/plan**n**ed

3 Verbs ending in a consonant + *-y* , change the *-y* to *-ied*.
study/stud**ied**   carry/carr**ied**

But …
play/play**ed**   enjoy/enjoy**ed**
There are many common irregular verbs. See the list on p85.

Use

The Past Simple expresses a completed past action. Notice some of the time expressions.

*We **played** tennis last Sunday.*
*I **worked** in London in 2007.*
*John **left** two minutes ago.*

 3.2 Past Continuous

Form

was/were + verb *-ing* (present participle)

Positive and negative

I/He/She/It	was wasn't (was not)	working.
You/We/They	were weren't (were not)	

Question

What	was	I he she it	doing?
	were	you we they	

	Short answer
Were you working yesterday?	***Yes, I was./No, I wasn't.***

Use

1 The Past Continuous expresses a past activity that has duration.
*I had a good time while I **was living** in Paris.*
*You **were making** a lot of noise last night. **Were** you **having** a party?*

2 The activity was in progress *before*, and probably *after*, a time in the past.
*'What **were** you **doing** at 8.00 last night?' 'I **was watching** TV.'*
*When I woke up this morning, the sun **was shining**.*

3.3 Past Simple and Past Continuous

1 The Past Simple expresses completed past actions. The Past Continuous expresses activities in progress. Compare these sentences.
*I **washed** my hair last night.*
*I **was washing** my hair when you **phoned**.*
*'What **did** you **do** at the weekend?' 'I **played** tennis.'*
*We **were playing** tennis when it **started** to rain.*

2 A Past Simple action can interrupt a Past Continuous activity in progress.
*When I **phoned** Simon he **was having** a shower.*
*I **was doing** my homework when Jane **arrived**.*

3 In stories, the Past Continuous can describe the scene. The Past Simple tells the action.
*It **was** a beautiful day. The sun **was shining** and the birds **were singing**, so we **decided** to go for a picnic. We **put** everything in the car …*

3.4 Prepositions in time expressions

at	in	on
at six o'clock at midnight at Christmas at the weekend	in 2007 in the morning/ afternoon/evening in summer in two weeks' time	on Saturday on Monday morning on Christmas Day on January 18th
no preposition		
two weeks ago yesterday evening this afternoon	next month tomorrow morning tonight	

UNIT 4

 4.1 Expressions of quantity

Count and uncount nouns

1 It is important to understand the difference between count and uncount nouns.

Count nouns	Uncount nouns
a cup	water
a girl	sugar
an apple	milk
an egg	music
a pound	money

We can say *three cups, two girls, ten pounds*. We can count them. We cannot say *two waters, three musics, one money*. We cannot count them.

2 Count nouns can be singular or plural.
*This **cup** is full.*
*These **cups are** empty.*

Uncount nouns can only be singular.
*The **water** is cold.*
*The **weather was** terrible.*

much and many

1 We use *much* with uncount nouns in questions and negatives.
*How **much money** have you got?*
*There isn't **much milk** left.*

2 We use *many* with count nouns in questions and negatives.
*How **many people** were at the party?*
*I didn't take **many photos** on holiday.*

some and any

1 *Some* is used in positive sentences.
*I'd like **some** sugar.*

2 *Any* is used in questions and negatives.
*Is there **any** sugar in this tea?*
*Have you got **any** brothers and sisters?*
*We don't have **any** washing-up liquid.*
*I didn't buy **any** apples.*

3 We use *some* in questions that are requests or offers.
*Can I have **some** cake?*
*Would you like **some** tea?*

4 The rules are the same for *someone, anything, anybody, somewhere*, etc.
*I've got **something** for you.*
*Hello? Is **anybody** here?*
*There isn't **anywhere** to go in my town.*

a few and a little

1 We use *a few* with count nouns.
*There are **a few biscuits** left, but not many.*

2 We use *a little* with uncount nouns.
*I only have **a little time**.*

a lot/lots of

1 We use *a lot/lots of* with both count and uncount nouns.
*There's **a lot of** butter.*
*I've got **lots of** friends.*

2 *A lot/lots of* can be used in questions and negatives.
*Are there **lots of tourists** in your country?*
*There isn't **a lot of butter**, but there's enough.*

 4.2 Articles – *a, an*, and *the*

1 The indefinite article *a* or *an* is used with singular, count nouns to refer to a thing or an idea for the first time.
*We have **a cat** and **a dog**.*
*There's **a supermarket** in Adam Street.*

2 The definite article *the* is used with singular and plural, count and uncount nouns when both the speaker and the listener know the thing or idea already.
*We have a cat and a dog. **The cat** is old, but **the dog** is just a puppy.*
*I'm going to **the supermarket**. Do you want anything? (We both know which supermarket.)*

Indefinite article
The indefinite article is used:

1 with professions.
*I'm **a teacher**.*
*She's **an architect**.*

2 with some expressions of quantity.
a pair of   a little   a couple of   a few

3 with expressions of frequency.
once a week   three times a day

4 in exclamations with *what* + a count noun.
***What** a lovely day!*
***What** a pity!*

Definite article
The definite article is used:

1 before seas, rivers, hotels, pubs, theatres, museums, and newspapers.
the Atlantic   the British Museum
The Times   the Ritz

2 if there is only one of something.
the sun   the Queen   the Government

3 with superlative adjectives.
*He's **the richest man** in the world.*
*Jane's **the oldest** in the class.*

No article
There is no article:

1 before plural and uncount nouns when talking about things in general.
I like potatoes.
Milk is good for you.

2 before countries, towns, streets, languages, magazines, meals, airports, stations, and mountains.
I had lunch with John.
I bought Cosmopolitan at Victoria Station.

3 before some places and with some forms of transport.

at home	in/to bed	at/to work
at/to school/university	by bus	by plane
by car	by train	on foot

*She goes to work **by bus**.*
*I was **at home** yesterday evening.*

4 in exclamations with *What* + an uncount noun.
***What** beautiful **weather**!   **What** loud **music**!*

Note
In the phrase *go home*, there is no article and no preposition.
*I went **home** early.*   NOT *I went to home.*

5.1 Verb patterns

Here are four verb patterns. There is a list of verb patterns on p87.

1   Verb + *to* + infinitive
    They **want to buy a** new car.   I'd **like to go** abroad.

2   Verb + *-ing*
    We **love going** to parties.   I **enjoy travelling** abroad.

3   Verb + *-ing* or + *to* + infinitive with no change in meaning
    It **started to rain/raining**.
    I **continued to work/working** in the library.

4   Verb + preposition + *-ing*
    We're **thinking of moving** house.
    I'm **looking forward to having** more free time.

like doing and *would like to do*

1   *Like doing* and *love doing* express a general enjoyment.
    I **like working** as a teacher. = I am a teacher and I enjoy it.
    I **love dancing**. = This is one of my hobbies.

2   *Would like to do* and *would love to do* express a preference now or at a specific time.
    I'd **like to be** a teacher. = When I grow up, I want to be a teacher.
    Thanks. I'd **love to dance**. = At a party. I'm pleased you asked me.

Question	Short answer
Would you like to dance?	*Yes, I would./Yes, I'd love to.*
Would you like to come for a walk?	*Yes, I would./No, thank you.*

Note
No, I wouldn't is not common because it is impolite.

 5.2 Future forms

will

Form

will + infinitive without *to*
Will is a modal auxiliary verb. There is an introduction to modal auxiliary verbs in Part B on p122. The forms of *will* are the same for all persons.

Positive and negative

I/He/She/It/You/We/They	'll (will) won't	come. help you. invite Tom.

Question
What time **will** *he/you/they* **be back?**

	Short answer
Will you help me?	*Yes, I will.*

Note
No, I won't is impolite. It means 'I don't want to help you.'
A polite way of saying 'no' here is '*I'm afraid I can't.*'
'*Will you give me a lift?*' '*Sorry,* **I'm afraid I can't.**'

Use

Will is used:

1   to express a future intention made *at the moment of speaking*.
    '*It's Jane's birthday.*' '*Is it?* **I'll buy** *her some flowers.*'
    I'll give you my phone number.
    '*Do you want the blue or the red pen?*' '**I'll take** *the red one.*'

2   to express an offer.
    I'll carry your suitcase.   We**'ll do** the washing-up.

3   to express a future fact. The speaker thinks it is sure to happen in the future.
    I'll be 30 next week.   **It will be** a nice day tomorrow.

This use is called the pure future. The speaker is talking about the future without expressing an intention, plan, or personal opinion.

going to

Form

am/is/are + *going* + *to* + infinitive

Positive and negative

I	'm (am) 'm not	
He/She It	's (is) isn't	going to leave.
You We They	're (are) aren't	

Question

When	am	I	going to arrive?
	is	he/she/it	
	are	you/we/they	

	Short answer
Are they going to get married?	**Yes, they are./No, they aren't.**

Use

Going to is used:

1   to express a future decision, intention, or plan made *before* the moment of speaking.
    How long **are** *they* **going to stay** *in Rome?*
    She **isn't going to have** *a birthday party.*

2   when we can see or feel now that something is certain to happen in the future.
    Look at these clouds! It's **going to rain**.
    Watch out! You're **going to drop** *that vase.*

will or *going to*?

Look at the use of *will* and *going to* in these sentences.

I'm **going to make** *a chicken casserole for dinner.*
(I decided this morning and bought everything for it.)
What can I cook for dinner? Er … I know! I'll **make** *a chicken casserole!* (I decided at the moment of speaking.)

Present Continuous

The Present Continuous for the future is used:

1   to express a planned future arrangement.
    I'm **meeting** *my cousin for lunch.*
    '*What* **are** *you* **doing** *this weekend?*'
    '*We're* **having** *a party. Can you come?*'

2   with the verbs *go* and *come*.
    She's **coming** *on Friday.*
    I'm **going** *home early tonight.*

Sometimes there is little or no difference between *going to* and the Present Continuous to express a future arrangement.
We're **seeing** *a film this evening.*
We're **going to** *see a film this evening.*

UNIT 6

 6.1 What ... like?

Form

what + to be + subject + like?

A ***What's*** *your teacher* ***like?***　　**B** *She's very patient.*
A ***What are*** *his parents* ***like?***　　**B** *They're very kind.*
A ***What*** *was your holiday* ***like?***　　**B** *Wonderful. We swam a lot.*
A ***What*** *were the beaches* ***like?***　　**B** *OK, but some were dirty.*

Note

1 We don't use *like* in the answer.
   She's patient.   NOT   ~~*She's like patient.*~~

2 *Like* in this question is a preposition, not a verb:
   'What's Jim ***like?***' '*He's intelligent and kind, and very good-looking.*'

3 In these sentences *like* is a verb:
   'What does Jim ***like?***' '*He* ***likes*** *motorbikes and playing tennis.*'

Use

1 *What ... like?* means 'Describe somebody or something. Tell me
   about it. I don't know anything about it.'

2 *How's your mother?* asks about health. It doesn't ask for a description.
   'How's your mother?' *'She's very well, thank you.'*

 6.2 Comparative and superlative adjectives

Form

1 Look at the chart.

		Comparative	Superlative
Short adjectives	cheap small *big	cheaper smaller bigger	cheapest smallest biggest
Adjectives that end in -*y*	funny early heavy	funnier earlier heavier	funniest earliest heaviest
Adjectives with two syllables or more	careful boring expensive interesting	more careful more boring more expensive more interesting	most careful most boring most expensive most interesting
Irregular adjectives	far good bad	further better worse	furthest best worst

*For short adjectives with one vowel + one consonant, double the
consonant: *hot/hotter/hottest; fat/fatter/fattest.*

2 *Than* is often used after a comparative adjective.
   I'm ***younger than*** *Barbara.*
   Barbara's ***more intelligent than*** *Sarah.*

   Much can come before the comparative to give emphasis.
   She's ***much nicer than*** *her sister.*
   Is Tokyo ***much more modern than*** *London?*

3 *The* is used before superlative adjectives.
   He's ***the funniest*** *boy in the class.*
   Which is ***the tallest*** *building in the world?*

Use

1 Comparatives compare one thing, person, or action with another.
   She's ***taller*** *than me.*
   London's ***more expensive*** *than Rome.*

2 We use superlatives to compare somebody or something with the
   whole group.
   She's the ***tallest*** *in the class.*
   It's the ***most expensive*** *hotel in the world.*

3 *As ... as* shows that something is the same or equal.
   Jim's ***as tall as*** *Peter.*
   I'm ***as worried as*** *you are.*

4 *Not as ... as* shows that something isn't the same or equal.
   She ***isn't as tall as*** *her mother.*
   He ***isn't nearly as clever as*** *me!*

Word list

Here is a list of most of the new words in the units of *New Headway Pre-Intermediate, Fourth edition* Student's Book.

adj = adjective	*pl* = plural
adv = adverb	*prep* = preposition
conj = conjunction	*pron* = pronoun
coll = colloquial	*pp* = past participle
n = noun	*v* = verb
opp = opposite	*US* = American English

UNIT 1

aboriginal *adj* /ˌæbəˈrɪdʒənl/
accident *n* /ˈæksɪdənt/
amazing *adj* /əˈmeɪzɪŋ/
another time /əˈnʌðə(r) taɪm/
art gallery *n* /ɑːt ˈɡæləri/
as many as /əz ˈmeni əz/
attractive *adj* /əˈtræktɪv/
blind date *n* /ˌblaɪnd ˈdeɪt/
borrow *v* /ˈbɒrəʊ/
Bulgaria *n* /bʌlˈɡeəriə/
charity *n* /ˈtʃærəti/
check-up *n* /ˈtʃek ʌp/
cheek *n* /tʃiːk/
Cheers! /tʃɪəz/
chopsticks *pl n* /ˈtʃɒpstɪks/
coach *n* /kəʊtʃ/
cosmopolitan *adj* /ˌkɒzməˈpɒlɪtən/
couple *n* /ˈkʌpl/
dates *pl n* /deɪts/
embarrass *v* /ɪmˈbærəs/
excited *adj* /ɪkˈsaɪtɪd/
first impressions *n* /fɜːst ɪmˈpreʃnz/
flat *adj* /flæt/
gang *n* /ɡæŋ/
Goodness! /ˈɡʊdnɪs/
greet *v* /ɡriːt/
Have a good weekend! /hæv ə ɡʊd ˌwiːkˈend/
hurry *n* /ˈhʌri/
impress *v* /ɪmˈpres/
interview *n* /ˈɪntəvjuː/
it doesn't matter /ɪt ˈdʌz(r)nt ˈmætə(r)/
journey *n* /ˈdʒɜːni/
mainly *adv* /ˈmeɪnli/
marathon *n* /ˈmærəθən/
Master's degree *n* /ˈmɑːstəz dɪˈɡriː/
messenger *n* /ˈmesɪndʒə(r)/
mistakes *pl n* /mɪˈsteɪks/
more and more /mɔː(r) ənd mɔː(r)/
my pleasure /maɪ ˈpleʒə(r)/
nervous *adj* /ˈnɜːvəs/
never mind /ˈnevə(r) maɪnd/
noise *n* /nɔɪz/
Not a great look! /ˈnɒt ə ɡreɪt lʊk/
nothing much /ˈnʌθɪŋ mʌtʃ/
notice *n* /ˈnəʊtɪs/
oldest *adj* /ˈəʊldɪst/
opening *n* /ˈəʊpənɪŋ/
percentage *n* /pəˈsentɪdʒ/
Pleased to meet you. /pliːzd tə ˈmiːt juː/
progress *v* /ˈprəʊɡres/

raisins *pl n* /ˈreɪznz/
readers *pl n* /ˈriːdəz/
reporter *n* /rɪˈpɔːtə(r)/
seat *n* /siːt/
shake *v* /ʃeɪk/
shapes *pl n* /ʃeɪps/
show round *v* /ʃəʊ ˈraʊnd/
Shut up! /ʃʌt ˈʌp/
signs *pl n* /saɪnz/
so many things /səʊ ˈmeni θɪŋz/
successful *adj* /səkˈsesfl/
sunshine *n* /ˈsʌnʃaɪn/
suppose *v* /səˈpəʊz/
survey *n* /ˈsɜːveɪ/
swap *v* /swɒp/
table manners *pl n* /ˈteɪbl mænəz/
terrible *adj* /ˈterəbl/
theatre *n* /ˈθɪətə(r)/
to have in common *v* /tə hæv ɪn ˈkɒmən/
train *v* /treɪn/
Turkish *adj* /ˈtɜːkɪʃ/
wear *v* /weə(r)/
wise *adj* /waɪz/
worry *v* /ˈwʌri/

UNIT 2

actually *adv* /ˈæktʃuəli/
afraid *adj* /əˈfreɪd/
architect *n* /ˈɑːkɪtekt/
article *n* /ˈɑːtɪkl/
average *n* /ˈævərɪdʒ/
behave *v* /bɪˈheɪv/
bright-red *adj* /braɪt red/
Cheer up! /tʃɪə(r) ʌp/
chill out *v* /tʃɪlˈaʊt/
clubs *pl n* /klʌbz/
currently *adv* /ˈkʌrəntli/
dance music *n* /dɑːns ˈmjuːzɪk/
deaf *adj* /def/
depend on *v* /dɪˈpend ɒn/
depressed *adj* /dɪˈprest/
download *v* /daʊnˈləʊd/
electro music *n* /ɪˈlektrəʊ ˈmjuːzɪk/
energetic *adj* /enəˈdʒetɪk/
enthusiastic *adj* /ɪnθjuːziˈæstɪk/
envious *adj* /ˈenviəs/
extraordinary *adj* /ɪkˈstrɔːdnri/
failures *pl n* /ˈfeɪljəz/
feel at home /fiːl ət ˈhəʊm/
festivals *pl n* /ˈfestɪvlz/
flavour *n* /ˈfleɪvə(r)/
fortune *n* /ˈfɔːtʃuːn/
gig *n* /ɡɪɡ/
grateful *adj* /ˈɡreɪtfl/
grow *v* /ɡrəʊ/
happiness *n* /ˈhæpinəs/
health *n* /helθ/
huge *adj* /hjuːdʒ/
image *n* /ˈɪmɪdʒ/
jars *pl n* /dʒɑːz/
jealous *adj* /ˈdʒeləs/
jogging *n* /ˈdʒɒɡɪŋ/
joy *n* /dʒɔɪ/
lie-in *n* /ˈlaɪ ɪn/
lipstick *n* /ˈlɪpstɪk/
major *adj* /ˈmeɪdʒə(r)/
marketing *n* /ˈmɑːkɪtɪŋ/
Mind your own business! /ˈmaɪnd jə əʊn ˌbɪznəs/
neighbours *pl n* /ˈneɪbəz/
obviously *adv* /ˈɒbviəsli/
on the way /ɒn ðə weɪ/
on their own /ɒn ðeə(r) ˈəʊn /
opportunity *n* /ˌɒpəˈtjuːnəti/
ordinary *adj* /ˈɔːdnri/
planning *n* /ˈplænɪŋ/
pleasure *n* /ˈpleʒə(r)/
products *pl n* /ˈprɒdʌkts/
relationship *n* /rɪˈleɪʃnʃɪp/
remarkable *adj* /rɪˈmɑːkəbl/
satisfaction *n* /sætɪsˈfækʃən/
saxophone *n* /ˈsæksəfəʊn/

score *n* /skɔː(r)/
secret *n* /ˈsiːkrət/
selling *n* /selɪŋ/
silver *n* /ˈsɪlvə(r)/
single *n* /ˈsɪŋgl/
smart *adj* /smɑːt/
stressed *adj* /strest/
suspicious *adj* /səˈspɪʃəs/
tea parties *pl n* /ˈtiː pɑːtiz/
tour *v* /tɔː(r)/
unemployed *adj* /ˌʌnɪmˈplɔɪd/
unusual *adj* /ʌnˈjuːʒəl/
young people *n* /jʌŋ ˈpiːpl/

UNIT 3

activate *v* /'æktɪveɪt/
admire *v* /əd'maɪə(r)/
adventure *n* /əd'ventʃə(r)/
adventurer *n* /əd'ventʃərə(r)/
appreciate *v* /ə'priːʃieɪt/
argument *n* /'ɑːgjəmənt/
beat *v* /biːt/
bite *n* /baɪt/
bleed *v* /bliːd/
cabin crew *n* /'kæbɪn kruː/
chute *n* /ʃuːt/
coast *n* /kəʊst/
companion *n* /kəm'pæniən/
crime *n* /kraɪm/
damage *v* /'dæmɪdʒ/
dangerous *adj* /'deɪndʒərəs/
dearly *adv* /'dɪəli/
endanger *v* /ɪn'deɪndʒə(r)/
enormous *adj* /ɪ'nɔːməs/
explode *v* /ɪk'spləʊd/
explosion *n* /ɪk'spləʊʒn/
fame *n* /feɪm/
fangs *pl n* /fæŋz/
flight attendant *n* /flaɪt ə'tendənt/
folk hero *n* /fəʊk 'hɪərəʊ/
forest *n* /'fɒrɪst/
forestry *adj* /'fɒrɪstri/
fountain *n* /'faʊntɪn/
furiously *adv* /'fjʊəriəsli/
guide *n* /gaɪd/
guns *pl n* /gʌnz/
half-time *n* /ˌhɑːf 'taɪm/
hammock *n* /'hæmək/
headline *n* /'hedlaɪn/
hostile *adj* /'hɒstaɪl/
injured *adj* /'ɪndʒəd/
jungle *n* /'dʒʌŋgl/
knives *pl n* /naɪvz/
land *v* /lænd/
length *n* /leŋθ/
locker *n* /'lɒkə(r)/
lost his cool /lɒst hɪz kuːl/
mend *v* /mend/
monkeys *pl n* /'mʌŋkiz/
overhead *adj* /'əʊvəhed/
PA system *n* /piː 'eɪ sɪstəm/
permission *n* /pə'mɪʃn/
quit *v* /kwɪt/
react *v* /ri'ækt/
record *v* /rɪ'kɔːd/
refuse *v* /rɪ'fjuːz/
robbery *n* /'rɒbəri/
runway *n* /'rʌnweɪ/
sleeping pill *n* /'sliːpɪŋ pɪl/
snake *n* /sneɪk/
source *n* /sɔːs/
star *v* /stɑː(r)/
strike *n* /straɪk/
sympathy *n* /'sɪmpəθi/
taxiing *v* /'tæksiɪŋ/
temper *n* /'tempə(r)/
terrified *adj* /'terɪfaɪd/
theft *n* /θeft/
thieves *pl n* /θiːvz/

tribe *n* /traɪb/
trip *n* /trɪp/
vase *n* /vɑːz/
web page *n* /'web peɪdʒ/
worldwide *adj* /'wɜːldwaɪd/

UNIT 4

allergic *adj* /ə'lɜːdʒɪk/
ambition *n* /æm'bɪʃn/
aspirin *n* /'æspərɪn/
automated *adj* /'ɔːtəmeɪtɪd/
beauty *n* /'bjuːti/
branches *pl n* /'brɑːntʃɪz/
breeze *n* /briːz/
broccoli *n* /'brɒkəli/
brochure *n* /'brəʊʃə(r)/
calorie *n* /'kæləri/
cans *pl n* /kænz/
chemist's *n* /'kemɪsts/
chewing gum *n* /'tʃuːɪŋ gʌm/
complain *v* /kəm'pleɪn/
connect *v* /kə'nekt/
coral *n* /'kɒrəl/
courage *n* /'kʌrɪdʒ/
crane *n* /kreɪn/
crystal-blue *n* /'krɪstl bluː/
dairy *n* /'deəri/
decaffeinated *adj* /ˌdiː'kæfɪneɪtɪd/
décor *n* /'deɪkɔː/
delicious *adj* /dɪ'lɪʃəs/
descend *v* /dɪ'send/
dessert *n* /dɪ'zɜːt/
diners *pl n* /'daɪnəz/
direct debit *n* /dəˌrekt 'debɪt/
disappointed *adj* /ˌdɪsə'pɔɪntɪd/
excitement *n* /ɪk'saɪtmənt/
expressions *pl n* /ɪk'spreʃnz/
fasten *v* /'fɑːsn/
fry *v* /fraɪ/
give (someone) a lift *v* /gɪv ə lɪft/
grill *v* /grɪl/
hang *v* /hæŋ/
heights *n* /haɪts/
help yourself /help jə'self/
homemade *adj* /ˌhəʊm 'meɪd/
honeymoon *n* /'hʌnimuːn/
industrial *adj* /ɪn'dʌstriəl/
lend *v* /lend/
limit *n* /'lɪmɪt/
loaf *n* /ləʊf/
loudly *adv* /laʊdli/
magical *adj* /'mædʒɪkl/
Maldives *n* /'mɔːldaɪvz/
mangoes *pl n* /'mæŋgəʊz/
meaning *n* /'miːnɪŋ/
nuts *pl n* /nʌts/
off-licence *n* /'ɒf laɪsns/
patent *n* /'peɪtnt/
pick up *v* /pɪk 'ʌp/
platform *n* /'plætfɔːm/
portion *n* /'pɔːʃn/
postman *n* /'pəʊstmən/
pots *pl n* /pɒts/
prawns *pl n* /prɔːnz/
programmer *n* /'prəʊgræmə(r)/
raw *adj* /rɔː/
restriction *n* /rɪ'strɪkʃn/
retire *v* /rɪ'taɪə(r)/
roast *v* /rəʊst/
robots *pl n* /'rəʊbɒts/
romantic *adj* /rəʊ'mæntɪk/

round *adj* /raʊnd/
seat belts *pl n* /'siːt belts/
sharks *pl n* /ʃɑːks/
shellfish *n* /'ʃelfɪʃ/
shopkeeper *n* /'ʃɒpkiːpə(r)/
sitting *n* /'sɪtɪŋ/
slices *pl n* /slaɪsɪz/
snack bar *n* /'snæk bɑː(r)/
software *n* /'sɒftweə(r)/
sparkling *adj* /'spɑːklɪŋ/
spectacular *adj* /spek'tækjələ(r)/
speechless *adj* /'spiːtʃləs/
spiral stairs *pl n* /'spaɪrəl steəz/
steam *v* /stiːm/
still *adj* /stɪl/
sting rays *pl n* /'stɪŋreɪz/
sunken *adj* /'sʌŋkən/
tap water *n* /'tæp wɔːtə(r)/
tip *n* /tɪp/
tonnes *pl n* /tʌnz/
touch-screen *n* /'tʌtʃ skriːn/
tropical fish *pl n* /'trɒpɪkl fɪʃ/
turtles *pl n* /'tɜːtlz/
underwater *adj* /ˌʌndə'wɔːtə(r)/
washing-up *n* /ˌwɒʃɪŋ 'ʌp/
weigh *v* /weɪ/
whisky *n* /'wɪski/

advertise *v* /'ædvətaɪz/
afterwards *adv* /'ɑːftəwədz/
amazed *adj* /ə'meɪzd/
apply *v* /ə'plaɪ/
arrange *v* /ə'reɪndʒ/
Belarus *n* /ˌbelə'ruːs/
billion *n* /'bɪljən/
biochemistry *n* /ˌbaɪəʊ'kemɪstri/
boomerang *n* /'buːməræŋ/
boss *n* /bɒs/
camping *n* /'kæmpɪŋ/
Capricorn *n* /'kæprɪkɔːn/
celebrate *v* /'seləbreɪt/
communicate *v* /kə'mjuːnɪkeɪt/
contaminate *v* /kən'tæmɪneɪt/
cycling *n* /'saɪklɪŋ/
debts *pl n* /dets/
delighted *adj* /dɪ'laɪtɪd/
disaster *n* /dɪ'zɑːstə(r)/
divorced *adj* /dɪ'vɔːst/
driving test *n* /'draɪvɪŋ test/
exams *pl n* /ɪg'zæmz/
experts *pl n* /'ekspɜːts/
fall out *v* /fɔːl 'aʊt/
farmers *pl n* /'fɑːməz/
fed up *adj* /ˌfed 'ʌp/
fluent *adj* /'fluːənt/
full-time *adj* /ˌfʊl 'taɪm/
get on *v* /get 'ɒn/
grown-up *adj* /ˌgrəʊn 'ʌp/
heavy *adj* /'hevi/
hope *n* /həʊp/
immediately *adv* /ɪ'miːdiətli/
jumper *n* /'dʒʌmpə(r)/
lawyer *n* /'lɔːjə(r)/
look after *v* /lʊk 'ɑːftə(r)/
look up *v* /lʊk 'ʌp/
lucky *adj* /'lʌki/
medicine *n* /'medɪsn/
miserable *adj* /'mɪzrəbl/
miss *v* /mɪs/
mushrooms *n* /'mʌʃruːmz/
nephew *n* /'nefjuː/
newsagent *n* /'njuːzeɪdʒənt/
nuclear *adj* /'njuːkliə(r)/
owe *v* /əʊ/
paramedic *n* /ˌpærə'medɪk/
petrol *n* /'petrəl/
philosophy *n* /fɪ'lɒsəfi/
phrase book *n* /'freɪz bʊk/
pick *v* /pɪk/
pretty good /'prɪti gʊd/
prime minister *n* /ˌpraɪm 'mɪnɪstə(r)/
produce *n* /'prɒdjuːs/
run out of *v* /rʌn 'aʊt ɒv/
regret *v* /rɪ'gret/
stressful *adj* /'stresfl/
supper *n* /'sʌpə(r)/
surfing *n* /'sɜːfɪŋ/
test *n* /test/
traffic jams *pl n* /'træfɪk dʒæmz/
warm welcome /wɔːm 'welkəm/

annoyed *adj* /ə'nɔɪd/
blond *adj* /blɒnd/
bring up *v* /brɪŋ 'ʌp/
busier *adj* /'bɪziə(r)/
busiest *adj* /'bɪziɪst/
calm down *v* /kɑːm daʊn/
career *n* /kə'rɪə(r)/
cheerful *adj* /'tʃɪəfl/
citizen *n* /'sɪtɪzn/
climate *n* /'klaɪmət/
creative *adj* /kri'eɪtɪv/
culture shock /'kʌltʃə ʃɒk/
customers *pl n* /'kʌstəməz/
darker *adj* /'dɑːkə(r)/
democratic *adj* /ˌdemə'krætɪk/
development *n* /dɪ'veləpmənt/
driest *adj* /'draɪɪst/
equator *n* /ɪ'kweɪtə(r)/
experience *n* /ɪk'spɪəriəns/
fair *adj* /feə(r)/
financial *adj* /faɪ'nænʃl/
florist's shop *n* /'flɒrɪsts ʃɒp/
foreign *adj* /'fɒrən/
friendly *adj* /'frendli/
generation *n* /ˌdʒenə'reɪʃn/
heartbreaking *adj* /'hɑːtbreɪkɪŋ/
hectic *adj* /'hektɪk/
herbal *adj* /'hɜːbl/
honest *adj* /'ɒnɪst/
humid *adj* /'hjuːmɪd/
incredible *adj* /ɪn'kredəbl/
intelligent *adj* /ɪn'telɪdʒənt/
investment *n* /ɪn'vestmənt/
Kenya *n* /'kenjə/
largest *adj* /'lɑːdʒɪst/
messy *adj* /'mesi/
mix up *v* /mɪks 'ʌp/
moody *adj* /'muːdi/
multicultural *adj* /ˌmʌlti'kʌltʃərəl/
nationality *n* /ˌnæʃə'næləti/
pharaohs *pl n* /'feərəʊz/
Philippines *n* /'fɪlɪpiːnz/
qualities *pl n* /'kwɒlətiz/
reliable *adj* /rɪ'laɪəbl/
religion *n* /rɪ'lɪdʒən/
reveal *v* /rɪ'viːl/
safe *adj* /seɪf/
salary *n* /'sæləri/
selfish *adj* /'selfɪʃ/
serve *v* /sɜːv/
shy *adj* /ʃaɪ/
skies *pl n* /skaɪz/
society *n* /sə'saɪəti/
South American *adj* /saʊθ ə'merɪkən/
surrounded *adj* /sə'raʊndɪd/
system *n* /'sɪstəm/
temperature *n* /'temprətʃə(r)/
thankful *adj* /'θæŋkfl/
tidy *adj* /'taɪdi/
twin *n* /twɪn/
wealthy *adj* /'welθi/
well-behaved *adj* /ˌwel bɪ'heɪvd/
wetter *adj* /'wetə(r)/

Pairwork Student A

UNIT 2 p16

PRACTICE

Speaking – exchanging information

3 Work with a partner. Answer questions about Ilona.

Ask questions about Bill and Christina. Complete the chart.

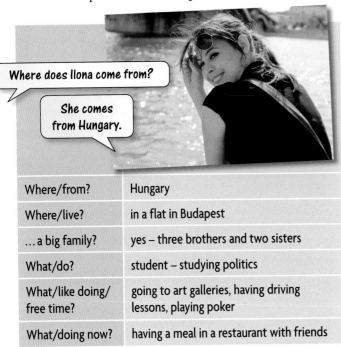

Where/from?	Hungary
Where/live?	in a flat in Budapest
…a big family?	yes – three brothers and two sisters
What/do?	student – studying politics
What/like doing/ free time?	going to art galleries, having driving lessons, playing poker
What/doing now?	having a meal in a restaurant with friends

Where/from?	
Where/live?	
…a big family?	
What/do?	
What/like doing/ free time?	
What/doing now?	

UNIT 5 p41

PRACTICE

When can we meet?

3 Work with a partner. Arrange to meet in the next week. Look at your diary.

	morning	afternoon	evening
Monday	study		meet Katie in town
Tuesday	study	visit Uncle Chris	
Wednesday	study		go to the cinema with Jenny
Thursday	study		cook meal for Mum and Dad
Friday	study	have piano lesson	

Pairwork Student B

 UNIT 2 *p16*

PRACTICE

Speaking – exchanging information

3 Work with a partner. Ask questions about Ilona. Complete the chart.

Answer questions about Bill and Christina.

Where does Ilona come from?

She comes from …

Where/from?	
Where/live?	
…a big family?	
What/do?	
What/like doing/ free time?	
What/doing now?	

Where do Bill and Christina come from?

They come from the United States.

Where/from?	the United States
Where/live?	in a house on the beach in LA
…a big family?	no – just one daughter
What/do?	Bill – IT consultant Christina – writes travel guides
What/like doing/ free time?	walking on the beach, going swimming, doing yoga
What/doing now?	shopping in a supermarket

 UNIT 5 *p41*

PRACTICE

When can we meet?

3 Work with a partner. Arrange to meet in the next week. Look at your diary.

What are you doing on Monday afternoon?

I'm playing tennis with Joe. Are you doing anything on Tuesday afternoon?

	morning	afternoon	evening
Monday	study	play tennis with Joe	
Tuesday	study		watch football at Dan's house
Wednesday	study	visit Tom in hospital	
Thursday	study		
Friday	study		

Extra materials

PRACTICE

Talking about the news

7 Choose one of the stories and read it. Make sure you understand all the words.

Work in small groups. Tell your story to the others. DON'T read it!
The other students can ask questions.

Texting woman falls into fountain

A woman who fell into a fountain while she was shopping is becoming an international hit on YouTube.

A video of her falling into the water went online last Friday, and since then 1.8 million people have watched it.

The woman was in a shopping mall in Nottingham in the UK. She was walking along the mall and texting at the same time, so she wasn't looking where she was going. Security cameras filmed her as she fell into a fountain. Fortunately the water wasn't very deep. When she climbed out of the fountain, she finished sending her text, then carried on walking down the mall.

Granny stops robbery

Janet Powell, a 71-year-old grandmother, yesterday stopped a robbery at a mobile phone shop in Birmingham.

At 9.30am Mrs Powell was doing her shopping. She heard a noise on the other side of the street. 'At first I thought it was a mugger,' she said, 'so I crossed the street. I wanted to do something to help.'

Then she realized that six men had hammers, and they were trying to smash the windows of a mobile phone shop. 'That made me more angry!' said Janet.

She attacked the men with her shopping bag, and shouted for help.

Police arrived and all six men were arrested.

Chinese vase sells for £53 million

A woman who lives in a suburb of north-west London was clearing out the house of her brother who recently died. She found a vase that her brother kept on a shelf in his dining room.

She said that her brother was very fond of the vase, although she didn't really like it herself.

A local antique shop thought it was worth about £800. So she asked an auction house to look at it, and they discovered it was from the Qianlong period, and dated it from the mid 18th century.

Yesterday it sold for £53 million to a Chinese buyer. The woman's son said that his mother was at first surprised, then amazed, then totally breathless.

The app that saved an iPad

A thief who stole an iPad led police straight to his door, as the owner had an app called 'Find my iPad'.

Ronald Bowe, 59, from Gateshead, stole the hand-held computer from a bag in St Nicholas's Cathedral, Newcastle, while its owner, Xin Shi, was praying.

Mr Xin reported the theft to the police, then realised he could use the app to find out where his iPad was. The GPS app gives the location of the computer.

Police followed the app to Bowe's house, where they found a bag containing the iPad, a mobile phone, a wallet, and a bank card.

Bowe was found guilty and will be sentenced at a later date.

READING AND SPEAKING

What do you think?

20 October

STEVEN SLATER ADMITS GUILT

The American flight attendant, who received world-wide attention in the summer and became a media and Internet sensation, appeared in court yesterday.

He admitted that he lost his temper, put the lives of passengers in danger, and caused damage to the plane when he activated the emergency chute.

Slater will have one year of counselling for anger management and treatment for alcohol abuse. If he doesn't complete the treatment, he could go to prison for one to three years.

He also has to pay a fine of $10,000 to JetBlue for damage to the plane.

Slater is currently unemployed.

WRITING – Building a story

A fishy tale

Ten days ago businessman, Andrew Cheatle, was walking on the beach near his home in Worthing, Sussex, when he lost his mobile phone. It fell into the water and unfortunately a wave took it out to sea. One week later fisherman, Glen Kerley, was on his boat catching fish to sell in the market. The same day, back on land, he was preparing the fish for sale when he noticed something metal inside a cod fish. It was a mobile phone. Glen couldn't believe it. The phone was smelly and dirty, but amazingly it still worked so Glen called some of the contact numbers. Soon he had a reply.

Andrew was out shopping for a new mobile phone with his girlfriend, Rita Smith, when her phone rang. Incredibly she said 'It's for you! It's a call from your phone.' Glen told Andrew the fishy tale of how he found the phone. They met the next day and he returned it to an amazed Andrew, who still uses it.

Glen Kerley   Andrew Cheatle

Irregular verbs

Base form	Past Simple	Past participle
be	was/were	been
become	became	become
begin	began	begun
break	broke	broken
bring	brought	brought
build	built	built
buy	bought	bought
can	could	been able
catch	caught	caught
choose	chose	chosen
come	came	come
cost	cost	cost
cut	cut	cut
do	did	done
drink	drank	drunk
drive	drove	driven
eat	ate	eaten
fall	fell	fallen
feel	felt	felt
fight	fought	fought
find	found	found
fly	flew	flown
forget	forgot	forgotten
get	got	got
give	gave	given
go	went	gone/been
grow	grew	grown
have	had	had
hear	heard	heard
hit	hit	hit
keep	kept	kept
know	knew	known
learn	learnt/learned	learnt/learned
leave	left	left
lose	lost	lost
make	made	made
meet	met	met
pay	paid	paid
put	put	put
read /riːd/	read /red/	read /red/
ride	rode	ridden
run	ran	run
say	said	said
see	saw	seen
sell	sold	sold
send	sent	sent
shut	shut	shut
sing	sang	sung
sit	sat	sat
sleep	slept	slept
speak	spoke	spoken
spend	spent	spent
stand	stood	stood
steal	stole	stolen
swim	swam	swum
take	took	taken
tell	told	told
think	thought	thought
understand	understood	understood
wake	woke	woken
wear	wore	worn
win	won	won
write	wrote	written

Verb patterns

Verb + -*ing*	
like	
love	swimming
enjoy	
hate	
finish	cooking
stop	

Note

We often use the verb *go* + -*ing* for sports and activities.

> I **go swimming** every day.
> I **go shopping** at the weekend.

Verb + *to* + infinitive	
choose	
decide	
forget	
promise	
manage	to go
need	
help	
hope	to work
try	
want	
would like	
would love	

Verb + -*ing* or *to* + infinitive	
begin	raining/to rain
start	

Verb + preposition + -*ing*	
think of	going
look forward to	

Modal auxiliary verbs	
can	
could	
must	go
had to	
shall	
should	arrive
will	
would	

Phonetic symbols

Consonants

1	/p/	as in	**pen** /pen/
2	/b/	as in	**big** /bɪg/
3	/t/	as in	**tea** /tiː/
4	/d/	as in	**do** /duː/
5	/k/	as in	**cat** /kæt/
6	/g/	as in	**go** /gəʊ/
7	/f/	as in	**four** /fɔː/
8	/v/	as in	**very** /ˈveri/
9	/s/	as in	**son** /sʌn/
10	/z/	as in	**zoo** /zuː/
11	/l/	as in	**live** /lɪv/
12	/m/	as in	**my** /maɪ/
13	/n/	as in	**now** /naʊ/
14	/h/	as in	**happy** /ˈhæpi/
15	/r/	as in	**red** /red/
16	/j/	as in	**yes** /jes/
17	/w/	as in	**want** /wɒnt/
18	/θ/	as in	**thanks** /θæŋks/
19	/ð/	as in	**the** /ðə/
20	/ʃ/	as in	**she** /ʃiː/
21	/ʒ/	as in	**television** /ˈtelɪvɪʒn/
22	/tʃ/	as in	**child** /tʃaɪld/
23	/dʒ/	as in	**German** /ˈdʒɜːmən/
24	/ŋ/	as in	**English** /ˈɪŋglɪʃ/

Vowels

25	/iː/	as in	**see** /siː/
26	/ɪ/	as in	**his** /hɪz/
27	/i/	as in	**twenty** /ˈtwenti/
28	/e/	as in	**ten** /ten/
29	/æ/	as in	**bag** /bæg/
30	/ɑː/	as in	**father** /ˈfɑːðə/
31	/ɒ/	as in	**hot** /hɒt/
32	/ɔː/	as in	**morning** /ˈmɔːnɪŋ/
33	/ʊ/	as in	**football** /ˈfʊtbɔːl/
34	/uː/	as in	**you** /juː/
35	/ʌ/	as in	**sun** /sʌn/
36	/ɜː/	as in	**learn** /lɜːn/
37	/ə/	as in	**letter** /ˈletə/

Diphthongs (two vowels together)

38	/eɪ/	as in	**name** /neɪm/
39	/əʊ/	as in	**no** /nəʊ/
40	/aɪ/	as in	**my** /maɪ/
41	/aʊ/	as in	**how** /haʊ/
42	/ɔɪ/	as in	**boy** /bɔɪ/
43	/ɪə/	as in	**hear** /hɪə/
44	/eə/	as in	**where** /weə/
45	/ʊə/	as in	**tour** /tʊə/

Notes

OXFORD
UNIVERSITY PRESS

Great Clarendon Street, Oxford, OX2 6DP,
United Kingdom

Oxford University Press is a department of the University of Oxford. It furthers the University's objective of excellence in research, scholarship, and education by publishing worldwide. Oxford is a registered trade mark of Oxford University Press in the UK and in certain other countries

First published in 2012
2017
10 9 8 7

ISBN: 978 0 19 476955 6 Complete Editon
ISBN: 978 0 19 476956 3 Student's Book A
ISBN: 978 0 19 476957 0 Student's Book B

Printed in China

This book is printed on paper from certified and well-managed sources.

ACKNOWLEDGEMENTS

The authors and publisher are grateful to those who have given permission to reproduce the following extracts and adaptations of copyright material: p.14 Fictitious interview with Mamy Rock (Ruth Flowers) and article based on factual information, www.mamyrock.com. Reproduced by permission; p.15 Fictitious interview with Fraser Doherty and article based on factual information, www.superjam.co.uk. Reproduced by permission; pp.66 & 67 From 'So what happened when two families swapped children?' by Tessa Cunningham, *Daily Mail* 11 August 2010. Reproduced by permission; pp.42 & 43 Interview with Palina Yanachkina is fictitious and is reproduced by permission of Palina Yanachkina. Article adapted from 'First person: Palina Yanachkina 'I have two families'' by Danielle Wrate, 5 May 2008, *The Guardian*. Copyright Guardian News & Media Ltd 2008. Reproduced by permission; pp.50 & 51 From 'The British Dream' by Tim Pozzi, 19 July 2008, timesonline.co.uk. Reproduced by permission of NI Syndication; pp.58 & 59 Article about Chatsworth reproduced by permission of the Chatsworth House Trust; pp.65 Interview with Jessica Ennis is fictitious and is based on factual information from *The Observer*, 15 November 2009. Reproduced by permission of JCCM Ltd; pp.82 & 83 Extracts adapted from 'A first time for everything' by Tom Meltzer, 23 October 2009, *The Guardian*. Copyright Guardian News & Media Ltd 2009. Reproduced by permission; pp.87 Information about Gareth Malone reproduced by permission of Curtis Brown; p.18 'Money' Words and Music by Berry Gordy JR and William Robinson JR © 1958. Reproduced by permission of EMI Music Publishing (WP) Ltd, London W8 5SW.

Sources: p.11 'Blind date' Source: www.guardian.co.uk; pp.26 & 27 'Emergency exit for flight attendant who lost his cool' Source: *The Evening Standard;* p.41 'I still can't believe I'm a grown-up!' Source: *The Times*; pp.26 & 27 'Steven Slater thanks public' Source: www.telegraph.co.uk/news

Additional information: p.63 Interview with Tilly Parkins is fictitious and is based on factual information; Tapescript 5.12 Fictitious interview with Palina Yanachkina reproduced by permission; Tapescript 8.1 Fictitious interview with Tilly Parkins is based on factual information. Tapescript 8.6 Fictitious interview with Jessica Ennis is fictitious and is based on factual information from *The Observer*, 15 November 2009. Reproduced by permission of JCCM Ltd.

Commissioned photography by: Gareth Boden pp.8 (man in street), 10 (Sally, Dominic, piano), 12 (dictionaries), 20, 31, 37, 46, 53 (leaflets/flyers), 54, 89.

Illustrations by: Ian Baker p.69; Fausto Bianchi/Beehive Illustration p.72; Gill Button pp.24, 29, 52, 68, 76, 81, 92; Katriona Chapman/The Bright Agency pp.70, 71; Simon Cooper/The Organisation pp.41, 44 (throw something away etc), 88; Tom Croft pp.13, 21 (John and Maria), 84, 101; Lucy Davey/The Artworks p.17; Maxwell Dorsey/Meiklejohn Illustration Ltd pp.16, 44 (look after a baby, etc.), 95; Penko Gelev pp.74, 75; Andy Hammond/Illustration p.106; Martin Sanders pp.22, 42, 60; Tony Sigley pp.26, 65, 59

We would also like to thank the following for permission to reproduce the following photographs: Alamy pp.8 (mobile phone/Mark Bassett), 18 (bubbles/Laurel), 28 (Photo Cornwall), 32 (fish & chips/numb), 33 (Fish and Chips sign/Mick Sinclair), 33 (shopkeeper/Trinity Mirror/Mirrorpix), 49 (Marilou/Jon Feingersh/Blend Images), 53 (Inca gold/Peter Horree), 56 (canoeing/TMI), 59 (long gallery/Ros Drinkwater), 60 (Alice Bews/Ian Shaw), 70 (Alice/Lebrecht Music and Arts Photo Library), 73 (Dr Jekyll and Mr Hyde/AF archive), 80 (ball-point pen/bobo), 80 (radio/Marc Arundale), 83 (Facebook/David J. Green – Lifestyle 2), 92 (couple/Andrey Kekyalyaynen), 93 (gravestone/Jeff Morgan 05), 107 (CJG – Lifestyle); By kind permission of Linda Barnicott, *My Hometown, Pittsburgh Remembered Series*, 1993/www.lindabarnicott.com p.62; Oliver Beatson, released on Public Domain licence on Wikipedia, 2009 p.99 (Life Cycle of the Sun); Camera Press, London pp.88 (young Charlotte Church/Paul Massey), 91 (young Jean Paul Getty III/Photography by Brian Aris), 131 & 132 (Charlotte Church/Sean Cook); Courtesy of Chatsworth House Trust pp.58 (D.Vintiner), 59 (dining room/D.Vintiner); Corbis pp.7 (Aboriginal art – blue painting/Ralph A. Clevenger), 9 (Zac/Simon Marcus/Comet), 9 (Katie and Beth older/Tim Hale Photography/Comet), 9 (Katie and Beth younger/moodboard), 16 (Bill and Christina/Philip Lee Harvey/cultura), 18 (parent and toddler/Ben Hupfer), 18 (meditating/Hans Huber/Westend61), 18 (child blowing/hsimages/Westend61), 25 (flood/Rehan Khan/epa), 25 (African children football/Christian Liewig/TempSport), 25 (crowd raising hands/Imaginechina), 25 (tents/Gideon Mendel For Action Aid/In Pictures), 25 (women queuing/Peter Turnley), 25 (earthquake rescue worker/WEDA/epa), 25 (footballers/Neil Marchand/Liewig Media Sports), 25 (helicopter/Rehan Khan/epa), 34 (Alexander/Bill Varie/Somos Images), 34 (Dinner in the Sky/Karoly Arvai/Reuters), 35 (man reaching at 's Baggers Restaurant/Daniel Karmann/epa/Corbis Wire), 38 (Tom/Rick Barrentine/Comet), 38 (Alison/Ocean), 39 (Bill/Beau Lark), 47 (Shanghai/Xiaoyang Liu/Flirt), 47 (Dubai/Jose Fuste Raga/Terra), 49 (Sally/Maskot), 58 (house and grounds/Peter Scholey/Robert Harding World Imagery), 60 (father and children/Ocean), 61 (Mika/Comet), 67 (football boots/Image Source), 70 (Hamlet/Bettmann), 70 (Oliver Twist/John Springer Collection), 70 (Sherlock Holmes/Bettmann), 73 (Charles Dickens/Bettmann), 73 (Robert Louis Stevenson/Bettmann), 80 (television/Lawrence Manning/Spirit), 80 (paper/Klaus Tiedge/Fancy), 82 (Henry/Blue Jean Images/Collage), 82 (background/ImageZoo), 91 (Jean Paul Getty II/Bettmann), 94 (Christine Schneider), 95 (Sigrid Olsson/PhotoAlto), 96 (Sam/Peter Muller/cultura), 97 (Tony and his dad/E. Audras/Onoky), 97 (Jimmy/Ocean), 60 (Norbert Schaefer), 62 (historical Pittsburgh/SuperStock), 103 (John F Kennedy/Ted Spiegel), 83 (Bill and Christina/Philip Lee Harvey/cultura), 84 (Bill and Christina/Philip Lee Harvey/cultura); Keith Ducatel – www.KeithDucatel.com pp.22, (Ed Stafford & jungle), 23 (Cho), 23 (Ed Stafford paddling); Jude Edginton – www.judeedginton.com pp.66 (the Cafearo & Tibbett families); Getty Images pp.6 (Anton/Zia Soleil/Iconica), 6 (New York/Fredrik Skold/The Image Bank), 7 (Rowenna/NWDA), 9 (Pete/Johner Royalty-Free), 9 (Judy and Kenny/Severin Schweiger/Cultura), 9 (Damian and Toby/Marcy Maloy/Photodisc), 12 (Jill Fromer/Photodisc), 14 (Ruth Flowers/Mark Ralston/AFP), 14 (jam pot/Peter Dazeley/Photographer's Choice), 16 (Ilona/Chev Wilkinson/Cultura), 18 (teenagers on beach/Image Source), 18 (canoeing/Erik Isakson), 18 (men chatting/Martin Barraud), 18 (couple working/Zero Creatives), 21 (businessman and woman/John Giustina/Iconica), 23 (snake/Mark Moffett/Minden Pictures), 23 (night/James p. Blair/National Geographic), 25 (world/Fry Design Ltd), 25 (press photographers/Christopher Pillitz/Reportage), 25 (leaders/AFP), 25 (reporter/Yellow Dog Productions), 25 (fashion/AFP), 25 (tennis/AFP), 27 (on beach/New York Daily News), 34 (Hans/Jupiterimages/Comstock Images), 34 (Lucy/Westend61), 35 (Ithaa Undersea Restaurant/Jon Nicholson), 35 (cutlery/Steve Wisbauer/Stockbyte), 36 (trolley foreground/Fuse), 38 (Abby/Stockbyte), 38 (Kelly/Mike Powell/Stone+), 39 (Martin/DreamPictures/Riser), 40 (Pete/Hill Street Studios/Harmik Nazarian/Blend Images), 40 (Debbie/WIN-Initiative), 41 (Leo/B2M Productions/Photodisc), 41 (Elsa/Hola Images), 41 (Dan/Dougal Waters/Photodisc), 42 (field background/Ingmar Wesemann), 43 (clover/Burazin), 45 (undecided woman/Hill Creek Pictures/UpperCut Images), 45 (hand and placards/Image Source), 47 (Singapore/Keith Mcgregor/Digital Vision), 48 (Agnes/Andreas Kindler), 48 (Kevin/Simon Wilkinson), 49 (Marcel/Jupiterimages/FoodPix), 49 (Jamie/Mark Scoggins), 50 (pavement/Richard Newstead), 55 (Karl Marx/Hulton Archive), 56 (Frieda Hoffmann/Vicky Kasal/Photodisc), 56 (jeep/Michael Poliza), 56 (Great Wall/Martin Puddy/Asia Images), 56 (desert/Patrice Hauser), 56 (archaeology in Egypt/Khaled Desouki/AFP), 60 (Victorian family/Nigel Dobinson/SSPL), 62 (Adam Pretty/Stone), 63 (Tilly Parkins/Adam Pretty), 63 (football/Ryan McVay/Photodisc), 63 (golf clubs/Stockbyte), 64 (Jupiterimages/Comstock Images), 65 (Jeff J Mitchell), 69 (doctor/Chris Whitehead/Digital Vision), 69 (stethoscope/Stockbyte), 77 (cinema/altrendo images), 77 (man clinging/Antonio R. Ramos/Flickr Select), 78 (discarded phones/SSPL), 79 (icons/Jim Snyder), 80 (Mac computer/SSPL), 82 (Sandy/PhotoAlto/Michele Constantini), 82 (Liz/Adrian Weinbrecht/Cultura), 82 (Barry/LWA/Riser), 85 (Clerkenwell/the Agency Collection), 88 (mature Charlotte Church/Gareth Cattermole), 90 (background/Gyro Photography/amanaimagesRF), 90 (Jean Paul Getty I/Hulton Archive), 91 (mature Jean Paul Getty III/Bruno Vincent), 91 (Balthazar Getty/Kevin Winter), 93 (baby/Rosemarie Gearhart/the Agency Collection), 93 (engagement/John Slater/StockImage), 93 (divorce/Peter Dazeley/Photographer's Choice RF), 96 (Lily/Lynn Koenig/Flickr), 96 (Annie/Marcy Maloy/Photodisc), 97 (Fiona/Cosmonaut Creative Media, LLC/Vetta), 99 (our Solar System/Stocktrek Images), 104 (Dougal Waters), 57 (Oliver Lopez Asis), 61 (Student/amana productions inc), 61 (paper background/Jill Fromer/Photodisc), 62 (Pittsburgh now/VisionsofAmerica/Joe Sohm), 108 (student/Andrew Rich), 108 (globe/Doug Armand/Photographer's Choice RF), 109 (Erik Dreyer), 151 (Ilona/Chev Wilkinson/Cultura), 131 (telephoning/Clerkenwell/the Agency Collection), 84 (Ilona/Chev Wilkinson/Cultura), 132 (telephoning/Clerkenwell/the Agency Collection), 133 (Nico Hermann); iStockphoto pp.7 (Aboriginal art Kangaroo/Paul Pegler), 11 (balloons/robstyle1), 11 (rice bowl/Floortje), 26 (panel pins/Chromatika Multimedia), 26 (cork board/sorendls), 27 (torn paper/Trevor Hunt), 27 (torn paper/Trevor Hunt), 27 (Jon Helgason), 35 (sky background/Peter Firus), 36 (shelves background/Vladimir Maravic), 43 (Belarus flag/popjop), 48 (crowd/jan kranendonk), 49 (paper family/maeroris), 49 (Rachel/Juanmonino), 50 (street sign/Alan eisen), 65 (Jamie Farrant), 67 (ballet shoes/millionhope), 70 (book/DNY59), 73 (pile of books/Alan Crawford), 73 (feather/ryan burke), 78 (globe/Edward Grajeda), 80 (ipad/TommL), 82 (Martin/ImageSource), 83 (virus/Philip Barker), 86 (page of music/Joanne Green), 86 (ribbon of notes/redfrog), 96 (genie/Ruslan Kokarev), 96 (lamp/Sergey Kulikov), 96 (smoke/Chanyut Sribua-rawd), 97 (signpost/scibak), 100 (notebook/Floortje), 62 (frame/Victor Martello); Mary Evans Picture Library p.55 (Dean Street – 19th century); Oxford University Press, Charles Dickens, *David Copperfield*, Oxford Bookworms Library, 2008 p.73; Courtesy of Ping Pong Ltd www.pingpongdimsum.co.uk p.10 (restaurant); Press Association Images pp.27 (planes/Rick Maiman/AP), 27 (press conference/Seth Wenig/AP), 78 (Martin Cooper/Eric Risberg/AP), 85 (Seth Wenig/AP); Rex Features pp.14 (Fraser Doherty/Nick Cunard), 35 (family at 's Baggers Restaurant/Action Press), 55 (blue plaque/Stuart Clarke), 79 (Goldstriker iphone/Stuart Hughes), 82 (Cyberia/Patrick Barth), 103 (Caroline Kennedy/Startraks Photo), 106 (Courtesy Everett Collection), 86 (David McHugh); Royalty-free pp.43, 98 (earth/Corbis), 104 (Goodshoot); Science Photo Library pp.80 (telephone/Sheila Terry), 80 (printing press/CCI Archives), 99 (Milky Way/Mark Garlick), 99 (background/Royal Observatory, Edinburgh/AAO), 99 (the universe/NOAO/AURA/NSF); Splash News p.26 (inside plane); Solo Syndication p.30; Adapted from listings published in *Time Out* Magazine. Logo reprinted by permission of *Time Out* p.53; Photographs of Gareth Malone © Twenty Twenty Television 2009 pp.86–87; Muir Vidler/The Times/NI Syndication pp.50 (Burkham Mehmet, Stroud Green Road shops), 51 (Ming Liang Chen, Mehul Shah, Luz-Elena Lamprea); By kind permission of Palina Yanachkina and the Quaid family/Press22/Sean Curtin pp.42–43.

Although every effort has been made to trace and contact copyright holders before publication, this has not been possible in some cases. We apologise for any apparent infringement of copyright and, if notified, the publisher will be pleased to rectify any errors or omissions at the earliest possible opportunity.

Your Faith

A popular presentation of Catholic belief

a redemptorist publication